Continuing
Your Education

Continuing
Your Education

3 4 5 5 3

Cyril O. Houle

PROFESSOR OF EDUCATION
THE UNIVERSITY OF CHICAGO

McGraw-Hill Book Company

NEW YORK   SAN FRANCISCO   TORONTO   LONDON

II

To David

Preface

This book is written especially for adults. It is designed to provide advice and suggestions for those men and women who have already established themselves and who now want to fit an organized learning activity into the pattern of their lives as profitably and pleasantly as they can. They know that they cannot adopt a completely new way of living or a drastic change in their habits of behavior. But they do hope that they (like millions of others) can enlarge the dimensions of their minds, build substantial and rewarding continuing interests, and increase their personal and social effectiveness. How do they go about doing so? What are the wise ways of learning?

In preparing this book, the answers to these questions have been drawn where possible from relevant research. Where research is silent, the author has relied either on the advice given by other books on this general subject or on his own quarter century of experience with adults who are trying to learn. Finally, 470 men and women now engaged in some form of purposeful study were consulted to find out how they had solved the problems they encountered. The book owes much to the advice and practical suggestions these successful adult students were able to offer, and liberal use of their remarks is made throughout the text.

Ultimately each person's pattern of learning is highly individual. He works out his own way of doing things and his own distinctive style. The 470 successful adult students were asked, "Under what circumstances do you find that you do your best studying?" Here are four of the answers:

By being alone in a very cool room.

By renting a room in a hotel where I can be completely cut off.

My own personal plan of attack is to get into a hot tub of water and stay there for hours.

I found the best time to study was in the middle of the night.

If these answers were all put together, it might seem that the best of all ways to study would be alone in the middle of the night in a hot tub of water in a cool hotel room. This fact is not necessarily true!

Every subject also presents its own special difficulties. We do not learn mathematics and literature and physics and sociology and history and typing in precisely the same way. Many special problems must be left to the guidance of the teacher.

But behind the special approaches of individuals or the distinctive requirements of each subject studied there lie some common elements: how to plan a program of study, how to read intelligently, how to write clearly and effectively, how to concentrate, how to remember, and how to master a skill. It is with such general matters that this book deals. In addition, special help is provided for those adults who are enrolled in organized courses. For example, there are sections on how to take part in discussions or how to pass examinations. Since purposeful education may be continued throughout adulthood in countless other ways, many of them are also mentioned in the pages of this book. The final chapter is devoted to suggestions about how each person may build his own lifetime learning plan. Any reader of these pages who is not particularly concerned about these specific matters may simply skip the discussion of them.

Various authors and publishers have given permission to quote from their works. Acknowledgment of their kindness is given at the appropriate places.

This book has profited from the advice and suggestions of many people. In particular, Donald A. Deppe and Mary Ellen Bell gave to the manuscript a detailed care which made it very much better than it would have been otherwise.

The study on which the book is based was made possible by a grant from the W. K. Kellogg Foundation.

Cyril O. Houle

Contents

Chapter **1**

A Beginning
Suggestion

The art of learning must itself be learned. To be an effective student, you must know the best ways of study, and why they are best. The aim of this book is to provide that information. Then, to make this knowledge meaningful in your own life, you must practice the appropriate methods until you use them so easily and naturally that you scarcely need to think about them. A painter may know a great deal about color, perspective, and design, but he is judged by the canvases he produces and how well they reflect his distinctive point of view. While painting, the artist improves his technique, and he profits thereby. Learning, like painting, is an active process. The more effective you are in using the right techniques, the more you will profit from your study.

You can start your practice even as you begin to read this book, for it, like most nonfiction books, should be read in a special way. Descartes [1], the great philosopher, suggested this method more than three hundred years ago in introducing one of his own works. Here are his words, somewhat condensed:

> I should wish the reader at first to go over the whole of this book, without greatly straining his attention, with the view simply of knowing in general the matters of which I treat. Afterwards, if

1

they seem to him to merit a more careful examination, he may read it a second time, in order to observe the connection of my reasonings, marking the places which he wishes to examine further, and continuing to read without interruption to the end. Then, if he does not grudge to take up the book a third time, I am confident he will find in a fresh reading the ideas which will help him to solve his own particular difficulties.[1]

"What," you may object, "read through a book three times! Sounds like a waste to me."

You may be right! No rule applies in the same way to everybody. If you try the method suggested by Descartes, however, you may be surprised by its effectiveness. Howard Y. McClusky [2], a modern American psychologist, has found that when people first skim and then read carefully, their total reading time is less than when they plow straight through the pages expecting to get all the meaning by a single reading. Most adults remember much more from using the method which Descartes advised than from merely going through a book once. If the technique of "skim-read-examine" for serious nonfiction books is best for most people, it is probably best for you.

Why is this true? There are at least two reasons, the first of which can be illustrated by a simple example. Suppose you were required to commit to memory the following twenty-two words: part, such, if, central, helped, you, to, idea, as, understand, larger, some, you, book, be, a, the, understand, of, each, will, whole. You could certainly fulfill this requirement if you wished to do so, though it might take you a long time to be able to recite all the words without repeating or omitting any of them.

---

[1] The reader who wishes to refer to the various sources cited will find a complete list of references at the end of the book.

Now suppose you were asked to memorize the following twenty-two words: if, you, understand, the, central, idea, of, some, larger, whole, such, as, a, book, you, will, be, helped, to, understand, each, part. You would find it much easier to learn this list than the earlier one. As you can see, the words are the same, but in the second list they have been arranged in a meaningful relationship. Since you can grasp the whole, you can remember each of the parts very much more rapidly and efficiently than you could when you did not see how they fitted together.

The author of a book usually does not present a series of disconnected facts or observations. In his introduction, he ordinarily gives an overview of what he plans to say. Since he must necessarily be very brief and general at that point, however, he can merely suggest what he intends to do. Only a reading of the book itself can reveal its full scope and dimensions. The reader who plods methodically along will build only a gradual and imperfect picture of the whole. The parts are not deeply understood because they are not seen in relationship to that whole.

But the reader who first moves rapidly through the book to get its central idea and structure can then do his basic reading with a much clearer idea of what he must master. Each of the parts is given a broader meaning for him because he sees how they all fit together. He also can identify those parts on which he must concentrate because they are crucially important or are especially difficult for him to understand.

The second reason why the three-part method is desirable is that it gives a reader three different ways of approaching a book. Walt Whitman [3] once wrote, "Books are to be call'd for, and supplied, on the assumption that the process of reading is not a half sleep, but, in the highest sense, an exercise, a gymnast's struggle; that the reader is to do something for himself. . . ."

Any single kind of exercise gradually grows monotonous. If you use just one way of reading a book to get its meaning, your attention may soon begin to wander. If you approach it from at least three different ways, the freshness and novelty of approach of each one will help you to maintain your interest.

Later in this book, there are further suggestions about how to do the three special kinds of reading. You will need to practice each one in order for it to become completely natural for you. For the time being, if you want to begin to improve your own art of learning even as you read, Descartes's advice provides a sufficient guide to the method.

Why not give it a try?

Right now!

Chapter 2

Why and How
Adults Learn

In how many different ways do you learn? How often do you purposefully try to gain a skill, to acquire new facts, or to achieve greater understanding and appreciation?

Not long ago, a great many men and women were asked these questions in a piece of research carried out by Sherman Sheffield [1]. He began by making a list of twenty-two different ways by which adults learn. Some of these methods were formal: taking classes, joining discussion groups, belonging to organizations with educational purposes, and attending conferences and lectures. Others depended on individual study: reading worthwhile books, watching educational television, visiting museums and art galleries, and listening to records. Some of these activities may be considered recreational rather than educational, but all of them usually result in increased knowledge or greater appreciation.

Each person was asked how often he took part in each activity, and on the basis of his answer, he was given a score. The highest possible mark was 196. A man or woman who reached that level would be one who took part to a high degree and for a long time in all the twenty-two activities which Sheffield chose. The low score was zero. A person who ranked that low would never use any of these ways to improve himself.

Nobody scored as low as zero or as high as 196, though if more people had been questioned, those limits might have been reached. The lowest score was 14, the average was 65, and the highest was 155. The scores were arranged in a fairly normal curve of distribution. Every one of the twenty-two activities was important in the lives of a large number of the people who answered.

OPPORTUNITIES TO LEARN

Sherman Sheffield's research demonstrates an important fact about which most people have been only generally aware.

The adult in modern society can and does use many methods to increase his skill, his understanding, and his sensitivity. The opportunities available to us are far greater than those available to our ancestors. Education is no longer just a matter of childhood schooling, but has become a lifelong, varied, and stimulating activity with great influence in the lives of many modern men and women.

One need only look around to see how rapidly the opportunities to learn are growing. Universities are enlarging their extension programs. Public schools are adding new evening classes. Libraries and museums are reaching out to serve more and more people. Churches, industries, and unions are introducing many cultural and training opportunities. Educational television stations are growing in number and lengthening the time they are on the air. Money spent for books is increasing more rapidly than is that spent for any other leisure-time activity. Everywhere one turns, there is a new zest for learning throughout life.

WHY ADULTS LEARN

Every person who takes part in any such learning activity does so for his own unique reasons. Guiding all the impulses toward learning of millions of people, however, is one central idea: *Education is the best way to develop the countless potentialities for growth which everyone possesses.* This idea is not new, but most people in the past had no chance to take advantage of it. They were poor; they were overworked; they lived in remote places; their inadequate diet made them listless; and (most important) they had not had enough schooling in childhood to give them basic learning skills. Most of the people in the world still have these handicaps, but ever larger numbers of adults are being freed of them and are using this new freedom to advance both themselves and their society.

Some people learn because they want to achieve a goal which will make their lives better. They want higher-paying and more satisfying jobs. They want to know how to be good husbands or wives, good parents, good homemakers, or good citizens. They want to know how to get along with other people, or how to enrich their leisure hours by more rewarding hobbies and amusements. They want to know how to carry out some special responsibility which life has brought, that of being, for example, a company executive, a shop steward, a foreman, a school board member, or a club president.

Some people learn because they enjoy the various processes of learning. They may belong to a discussion group because they are stimulated by the vital interchange of opinion among several minds. They may go to a lecture because they like to hear a particular subject outlined with authority, directness, and clarity. They may read a great deal, and therefore always try to have plenty of books on hand.

Some people learn simply because they want to know. They have a passion for literature, for the theater, for philosophy, for history, for photography, or for any of the thousands of other aspects of human knowledge. Such people seek no practical rewards. The sheer joy of knowledge or understanding or accomplishment is all they want.

There may be other reasons for learning than these. Probably, however, the great majority of the people taking part in various learning activities do so primarily because they want to reach a goal, because they enjoy the act of learning, or because they simply want to know. Most of the others who study do so because of some combination of these three basic reasons.

Anybody interested in thinking further about the purposes of education will find a rich body of literature awaiting his exploration. One of the most useful sources is a wise and beautifully written book by Virginia Voeks [2] called *On Becoming an Educated Person*. While her observations are intended for college students, her comments and suggestions also have relevance for adults.

RANDOM AND PURPOSEFUL LEARNING

Most of the facts, habits, ideas, notions, and attitudes that people acquire come to them from random learning. A busy adult works, reads, talks with people, watches television, listens to the radio, sees movies, travels, and reflects. Every day he becomes a bit different from what he was the day before. As Theodore Roosevelt put it, "What I am to be I am now becoming."

Random learning occurs constantly in the life of everyone. We learn new facts from many sources. We learn new skills as the opportunity or need for learning them is presented to us: a new tool to make work easier or faster, a new gadget for the home, a new refinement on the car, a new game or dance step, or a way of overcoming a new obstacle. (A right-handed woman who breaks her right arm will learn surprisingly rapidly to get along with her left one.)

Life brings new understandings, too. Before we have children, we may assume that a crying baby is just a bother; after we have them, we know that the crying has a cause. We learn very quickly to understand also any special tone of voice of our loved ones and how they use certain words. (A mother who wishes to speak only good of everything will call anything she doesn't really like "interesting" or "different." Her family soon enough learns what she means!)

But random experience does not ordinarily permit anyone to go very deeply into any field of knowledge. A child born in Paris will learn to speak French without having any choice in the matter or ever purposefully deciding to learn it. But if he wants to understand his language, he will need to study it. Abraham Lincoln learned the speech of Illinois where he was raised, but his biographer, Benjamin Thomas [3], tells how hard he struggled to master his native tongue:

> ... the self-taught man who once would have given all he owned and gone in debt for the gift of lyric utterance had touched the summits of eloquence. Yet this, like his other achievements, had not come by mere chance. Patient self-training, informed reflection, profound study of a few great works of English literature, esteem for the rhythmic beauty that may be coaxed from language, all these had endowed him with the faculty to write well and to speak well, so that at last, when profound emotions deep within him had felt the impulse of new-born nobility of purpose, they had welled forth— and would well forth once more—in imperishable words.

We learn from experience chiefly in terms of what we bring to it. Oscar Wilde [4] once remarked that Rome was crowded with people "who go about with depressing industry, looking at everything and seeing nothing. . . ." Sometimes people do not look, sometimes they look but do not see—but sometimes they do see. The difference lies chiefly within them. How alert, how sensitive, and, most of all, how purposeful are they in seeking what they want to find? It is possible to turn over the pages of a book without getting its meaning. It is possible to go to a symphony concert and sit idly through the music, never trying to understand what the composer was trying to do, caring nothing about how he used his major themes and the instruments by which they are expressed, and failing to put him into any relationship with other composers.

Experience without purpose can fill the mind with a rich treasure of facts and associations and provide countless starting points for development—and yet leave everything all jumbled together. The mind becomes something like a great storehouse, filled with goods in disordered heaps, some in bright light, the rest in shadowy darkness. The person with such a mind has "learned" a large number of facts, but what he knows has no focus, balance, proportion, or perspective. Lord Macaulay [5], the English historian, once said about another man, "He half knows everything." We might respect this judgment more if someone else [6] had not, in turn, said about Macaulay that he "not only overflowed with learning but stood in the slop."

The wise person tries to have a great many different kinds of experience just because he wants to enlarge his ideas and his awareness of the wonderful diversity life offers. Such a desire itself provides a kind of purpose, though the learning to which it leads is not developed in any highly focused way. But in the life of everyone there should also be continuing and orderly efforts to enlarge the understanding, to know new facts, or to improve abilities. As Seneca [7], the wise old Roman, put it: "Nobody ever became wise by chance." Whatever the wish of the learner, the rewards of learning can be very great. Those who hope to achieve goals very often do so. Those who enjoy the process of learning get great satisfaction from their efforts. And those who seek only to know find that learning is its own reward.

ABILITY TO LEARN

The opportunity and the desire to learn, though necessary, are not enough. In addition, there must be the ability to choose suitable goals and to know how to go about reaching them. Although many people find great satisfaction in study, the experience is frustrating and unhappy for others. Three examples may serve to illustrate this point:

Mrs. Sutherland suddenly finds herself a widow at the age of forty-three. In addition to her grief, she must face the fact that she has to earn her living to support herself and her two teen-age children. Twenty years ago she had been a teacher, but her certificate has long since expired. She decides to use her insurance money to pay her expenses while she takes a refresher course to bring herself up to date on teaching procedures. At first the course seems promising, but after a while it all becomes a muddle. She cannot keep her attention on what she is studying, she fails examinations, and she is unable to hold the attention of the children when she does practice teaching. Presently, as she sees her insurance money being used up, she leaves the refresher course and takes the first job she can find, even though it is far beneath her capacity and pays less than she could make as a teacher. Her son and daughter manage to finish high school, but although they are bright, they have no hope of going on to college. And so their lives, and those of their children, are influenced by the fact that Mrs. Sutherland was not able to make a success of her refresher course.

Mr. Bergan, on the other hand, is a great success in business. He has worked hard, with single-minded devotion, filling up twelve-hour days and seven-day weeks for twenty-seven years. Now at the age of forty-six, he suddenly takes stock of himself—and he does not like what he sees. All he knows is his business, though he knows that thoroughly. But what is he getting out of life other than the pleasure of making more and more money? What should he do? Well, Churchill and Eisenhower found great satisfaction in painting. So he buys a lot of equipment, joins a class, and plunges into action. But everything he does looks messy. He just doesn't seem to have the knack. So, after two weeks, he quits. What about music? He engages a piano teacher, rents a piano, and starts off with a fine surge of energy. Another two weeks—and another dropout, this time because it is all just too complicated! What about philosophy? He stops in at a bookstore, chooses several volumes the clerk recommends, and settles down that evening with the one that looks most interesting. He reads along, sentence by sentence, trying to understand each thoroughly. By the middle of the third page, his eyelids droop. He tries again the next night. The same result. Presently the books go on the shelf, and he goes on to sports and hobbies. But none of them—not golf, not photography, not skin diving, not tropical fish, not gem cutting—holds his interest for long. Presently he gives up and goes back to his twelve-hour day and his seven-day week. Nine years later he has a heart attack. From then on, he has two concerns: his business and his health. Soon after he retires, he dies.

One day at the morning *Kaffeeklatsch*, Mildred Davis announces she is sick of life in the suburbs. It is all just too routine. House and family, church and shopping, television and movies—and a three-week vacation visiting the rest of the family once a year. "Is this all there is to life?" she demands. Her two friends put down their cups and ask what more she wants. "Some intellectual stimulation for one thing," she answers. What does she have in mind? Well, frankly, she has nothing in mind, but as the three begin to speculate about what they could do, Frieda Smithers comes up with the idea that they, plus some friends, might form a club and meet—say, once a month—in each other's homes. Each member in turn could take the responsibility for a program. As they discuss the idea and think about the other women they might involve, enthusiasm grows. Before very many days, the new group is an accomplished fact. One of the husbands suggests it ought to be called the Get-Together-and-Gab Club. To his surprise, his suggestion is promptly adopted. For a while, the idea is carried forward with high enthusiasm, but in the middle of the second year, it begins to be harder and harder to get anyone to take responsibility for a program. First one meeting, then another, then another has to be skipped. Finally, without anybody really knowing why or how it happened, the club has gone out of existence. Back to routine.

Thousands of little dramas like these are played out day after day. Every case is complicated and unique, but the cause of failure is the same in each. An individual or a group did not know *how* to learn. The desire was present and the resources were available. But Mrs. Sutherland, Mr. Bergan, and the Get-Together-and-Gab Club (like countless other women, men, and groups) did not know how to bring about the results they wanted.

FIRST SHARPEN YOUR AX

Most of the people who fail do not realize that they have not used a proper approach to learning. If asked, they would say they failed because they didn't concentrate enough or they didn't have sufficient self-discipline or they didn't have enough time or they were too busy or they were too old. These reasons all have just enough truth to make them seem convincing.

But millions of people of all ages and with limited time and talent are happily succeeding in their studies. These people have realized that effective learning requires the use of appropriate methods. Nobody expects to be a good golfer, tennis player, public speaker, or pianist without studying technique. Why should anybody expect that by mere will power he can force his mind or his body to learn?

The value of special training in methods of study has been proved again and again. Some years ago, Luella Cole Pressey [8] gave a course in this subject to fifty students who were failing their courses at Ohio State University. Another fifty students just like the first group did not get the training. When she checked almost four years later, she discovered that 58 per cent of those who had had the course had achieved a satisfactory grade record. Only 18 per cent of the untrained students had done so. Many other studies since then have shown the value of how-to-study courses, particularly because they have improved greatly since Luella Cole Pressey's pioneer effort.

Some college students with high grades do not use the most effective techniques, but succeed because of intelligence, special ability, or the expenditure of a great deal of time. When they do learn how to take fullest advantage of their talents, however, their learning accomplishments are higher than before. Even a person who is very efficient in his study habits can always find room for improvement.

Adults ordinarily have less time for study than college students and therefore need skill in learning even more than they do. Every hour must be made to count. The usual affairs of life, however, give no training in such skill and even cause it to deteriorate. Mrs. Sutherland must once have had some ability as a student, or she never could have secured a degree and been a successful teacher—but twenty years later she was out of practice. Without recognizing that fact, she tried to pick up just where she had left off. If the skill had been tennis, golf, or piano playing, she would have known she had to regain her technique before she could perform as well as she formerly did. Why should she not expect to do the same when she resumed study?

Some people never stop learning and therefore never get out of practice. Those who do stop and then want to start again must recognize their need to regain their ability. They should heed the advice of the woodsman who once said, "If you have to cut down a tree in ten minutes, spend the first two sharpening your ax."

ROUTE 25

The best way to learn how to study is suggested by a story often told by C. F. Kettering [9], the imaginative pioneer of the automobile business:

> My home is in Dayton, and we have had our laboratories for years in Detroit, which is several hundred miles away. I keep my home in Ohio and drive back and forth weekends. Some of the people who work with me also drive between Dayton and Detroit. One said, "I understand you drive from here to Dayton in 4½ hours."

> I said, "I can do that once in a while, depending on traffic."

> He said, "I don't believe it."

> I said, "But I do it."

He said, "I'm a much better driver than you are, and I can't do it."

I said, "I'm going down Friday. Why don't you ride along with me?"

So we rode into Dayton in about 4½ hours, or a little more, and he said, "Hell, no wonder you can do it. You didn't stay on Route 25!"

Now Route 25 is the red line that is marked on all maps between Detroit and Dayton. If you are a stranger, that's the road you should take. It never occurred to my colleague that you could take any other road on either side of Route 25. There's a lot of country on either side of it; in fact, half the earth is on each side of it.

The aim of this book is to smooth the beginning way so that the reader's desire to learn can gain power and assurance. The suggested rules, like Route 25, provide a useful guide for those who don't know the country, but the rules are not inflexible. They are intended to serve as guides, not as grooves. They must all be tested and tried, combined and grouped into a way of work which best suits the individual who uses them. Sometimes it is a lot of fun to explore the half of the earth which lies on either side of Route 25. And you may find there a faster road to your particular destination.

Chapter 3

Seven Keys to Effective Learning

Once in ancient times, a spoiled young king decided to learn geometry, which was then new and very much in vogue. But when his tutor began to reveal the mysteries to him, the king found them hard to understand. He demanded that he be taught not in the usual way but in a fashion appropriate to his station in life. "Sire," the wise man answered, "there is no royal road to geometry."

There is no royal road to anything really worth knowing. Learning can be enjoyable, engrossing, and challenging. Some ways of teaching or of studying are easier than others. And one can occasionally get a surface familiarity with a subject without exerting very much effort. But any learning that is worthwhile requires sustained endeavor, and, in the course of it, there are bound to be times of strain, of darkness, of confusion, or even of a sense of futility. A man who climbs a mountain expects difficulties, but they are all made worthwhile by the exhilaration of the moment when, at last, he stands on top, free and clear, with a great panorama spread before him, which he would never have seen if he had not put forth the effort. In the same way, anyone who wishes the rewards and the exhilaration which come from learning must work for them.

But while there is no royal road to the mountain top, seven key principles will greatly aid your effort to reach whatever summit of learning you may choose as your goal.

1. ACT AS THOUGH YOU ARE CERTAIN TO LEARN

Nothing so disturbs the beginning adult student as the nagging fear that he will not be able to learn what he would like to know. Nothing is more reassuring than the discovery through experience that he can succeed. Here is the testimony of two men and two women who have learned this lesson:

> Going back after a lapse of time, I was fearful and tense, but that is past.

> My worries lasted only for the one course—after that it became easier. It had been twenty-five years between courses. After receiving a D, I got mad—and now get A's and B's.

> My biggest problem was convincing myself that I could once again maintain a good average in my classes. I felt that I had forgotten how to study effectively. This fear only lasted for the first semester. Once I was convinced that I could keep up, my problem was solved.

> I resumed my study many years after I graduated from a Japanese university. The difference of the language, the customs of the colleges, and the background knowledge added to the difficulty of resuming the study. All these reasons and my shortness of time made me feel an inferiority complex at first and made me nervous. I tried to persuade myself that I had to have confidence from

my experience and good grades. But the most important thing was to go through the first semester. The second was easier, and I could regain my own tempo. I wasn't so nervous any more.

Let it be said at once that not everybody can learn everything. People differ from one another in intelligence, bodily strength, dexterity, and special abilities. Only a limited number of people can understand advanced mathematics, play the violin like Heifetz, write novels as well as Tolstoy, or have the philosophical insight of Aristotle or Spinoza. Few adults aspire so high. They know that such talents are extraordinary, and therefore do not worry about not possessing them. What is troubling to many men and women, however, is the fear that they do not have the ability to learn what normal people want to know.

If you have this fear, it may arise from one of two causes. You may think you are no longer as good a learner as you were when young. Or you may believe that some important element has been left out of your makeup—that you do not have enough intelligence to understand difficult ideas or that you have no capacity for a particular subject such as foreign language, mathematics, art, or music. Let us take up these two causes of worry, one after the other.

The relative learning ability of young people and adults has been studied by many investigators. The essential results of this research are: *Adults can learn most things better than children, though it may take them longer to do so.*

Children have some advantage over adults in learning those skills which require physical dexterity or bodily strength. Even here, however, adults can usually learn if they want hard enough to do so. (Many very old men and women have learned to care for themselves again after a stroke which everyone thought would cripple them forever.) Young people also have some advantage if sheer memory is the issue or if the subject matter to be mastered is not particularly meaningful. Adults may have special difficulty if what they want to learn goes against long-practiced habits. For example, the speaking of English makes one learn to use the lips, the tongue, the teeth, and the mouth in certain ways. The speaking of French requires that they be used in different ways. An adult who has been practicing English speech habits for forty years will therefore not be able to learn to speak French as readily or as perfectly as will a child who has been practicing English for only ten years.

These are relatively minor qualifications. For most things adults want to know, their maturity, their wealth of association, their breadth of awareness, and their disciplined use of their powers make them able to learn even more effectively than they did when they were children. Irma Halfter [1] has found, for example, that women over forty who took courses at two universities received higher grades than did the young women (between eighteen and twenty-five) who took the same classes. This advantage was maintained regardless of the subject, the instructor, or the method of teaching.

The adult learners consulted in writing this book also provided a wealth of support for the belief that adults can learn. Here is what five of them had to say:

I had stopped formal studying for a period of fifteen years and upon resumption was quite surprised that the habit of learning was so easy to resume. Instead of finding special problems, I found it less difficult—whether this represented a maturity on my part, or settled habits, or better powers of concentration, I could not evaluate.

I find learning easier as an adult because I have a more intense desire to acquire new knowledge and explore ideas. Understanding comes easier.

Learning comes easier today because the years have taught me to analyze problems better and come up with better solutions.

After twenty years, I found learning easier. I concentrated better, was more interested—consequently learned more.

I felt more mature and in a better position to cope with what I wanted to learn.

Such evidence as the foregoing is often not convincing to an adult who is starting out on a program of learning, doggedly certain that he is doing very poorly. He simply cannot learn as well as he did when young, he believes, and it does very little good to quote statistics or inspiring statements to him. For he is probably right. He really cannot do as well as he did when he stopped studying twenty years before, but his difficulty comes not because he is old but because he is out of practice. He needs time to work his way back up to his former level of excellence, as so many others have done before him. He must hold fast to the idea that he *can* get back to that level and that he is not forever barred from doing so because he is too old!

Now to turn to a second possible worry: that you simply do not have the basic capacity to learn what you want to know. You may be right. If so, there is no point in putting yourself under undue strain. If basic inadequacy is your persistent and continuing worry, your best course of action is to try to get a specialized diagnosis of your ability. Consult a counselor, discuss your problems with a teacher, or make arrangements to take the appropriate tests of your aptitude. Then act in terms of what you discover.

Most adults, however, tend to underestimate their ability. They vaguely fear they do not have the capacity to absorb what they want to know. To them one can only say, "How do you know you can't learn unless you try?" Few people become absolute masters of any subject; the great majority fall somewhere short of perfection and yet gain pleasure in what they *have* learned. If you really try to learn in the most effective way, perhaps you will discover that far from having a blind spot in foreign language or mathematics or human relations, you can secure a real sense of satisfaction in studying them, partly because of your new knowledge and partly because you have conquered your fears. Of all the boundaries of the mind, the most limiting are those which it imposes on itself.

The first and basic rule, then, is to act as though you are certain to learn. There will be dark moments and even dark days—but they will pass. Somehow, by acting as though you were confident, you really will become confident. In an old play, a mother is talking to her shy daughter who is going off to her first ball and is dreading the experience. "My dear," she says, "bite your lips to make them nice and red, throw your shoulders back, hold your head high—and sail right in!" The beginning student may not need red lips, but the rest of the advice is helpful.

2. SET REALISTIC GOALS—AND MEASURE THEIR ACCOMPLISHMENT

One frequent obstacle to adult learning is that men and women, realizing that they have the full power of their strength and vigor, think that they ought to be able to learn without any effort or strain whatever.

Let us return to Mr. Bergan, whom we met in the last chapter, and his attempt to play the piano. He sees how much pleasure his friends get from playing. He is a very successful man, perhaps even better at business than they are. Subconsciously and without intending to do so, he really thinks of himself as already being able to play. Rationally he knows he will have to practice, but even as he thinks of it, he passes it over quickly in his mind. He will soon be as good as his friends. He, too, will be the center of attention at parties, when everyone gathers around him at the piano and harmonizes. So he moves forward at full speed.

At once everything begins to seem frightfully complicated. The keys are known by letters. They have been arranged on the keyboard in a wholly irrational fashion. (Why is the middle key with which he begins marked *c;* why is it not *a?*) He is expected to read from a novel arrangement of lines and spaces, in which every little mark means something. Each key must be struck with the appropriate finger; it must be hit at the right time and in the right order, and presently he must keep both hands going at once. Then he must leave the safe refuge of the white keys and begin to use the black. Soon he needs to pedal. Even after all that, the difference between his playing and that of his friends is phenomenal. Maybe, after all, you can't teach an old dog new tricks—

Now, a forty-six-year-old can probably learn to play the piano almost as rapidly and well as a ten-year-old, given exactly the same instruction and the same number of hours of practice. (As for the old proverb about dogs, it isn't true; an eight-and-a-half-year-old Irish terrier of the author's acquaintance learned two new tricks last summer.) But the child takes it for granted that he will have to practice. Somehow the adult hopes to be exempt from the rule. His goal is so clear-cut! His powers are so great!

If a man and a boy start out to walk a mile, the man will do it much more efficiently than his companion. He is tall enough to see the objective; he has a clear idea of what a mile's distance is and he can pace his progress accordingly; he keeps steadily at his task; and he is strong. The boy cannot see where he is going; he has no real conception of what the word *mile* means; he makes many side excursions; he runs too hard and gets a side ache, or he lags behind; his mind is easily diverted; and his legs are not used to the task assigned. Thus, the man will always be more efficient. But the mile to be walked remains. There is no royal road to learning.

In any learning program, therefore, you must first of all be realistic about what you can achieve. Do not start impulsively on an ambitious reading program, register by mail for an evening school course about which you are poorly informed, purchase a lot of equipment to teach yourself a hobby you are not really convinced you want to learn, or start on a program to get a degree because of a vague belief that it would be nice to have one.

If you are learning because you want to reach some goal, be sure that you really want it; be sure that what you want to learn will help you to reach it; be sure that you want to take on the task of learning. If you are participating in an educational activity because you enjoy doing so, be sure that the activity you choose will give you the satisfactions you want. (If you like to belong to discussion groups, for example, choose groups which really do discuss, which deal in interesting topics, and which are made up of congenial people.) If you learn because you want to know, be sure that what you choose will contribute to your knowledge in the way that you wish.

Having chosen your broad objective and selected the activity which will help you reach it, keep setting specific goals for yourself. As one man remarked, "I always plan ahead and know each night what I expect to accomplish, and when, the next day. I try to adhere to my daily plan." Even the largest building must be built one brick at a time. Some adults are very inventive in planning ways to set up short-range targets. They make each chapter a goal; they work against the clock to see how much can be accomplished each hour; they keep a ledger recording their plan on the debit side and their accomplishment on the credit side; or they divide up a job to be done into separate parts, each of which can be finished in a set period of time or before an established deadline.

Specific goals are important because they provide a feeling of tangible achievement. As one woman explained, "Each lesson well done brings its own rewards." Anyone who feels a sense of accomplishment and who recognizes that he has already gone a part of the way toward the broad goal at which he is aiming has a powerful incentive to continue.

Some adults like to arrange rewards for themselves other than the satisfaction which learning brings. They promise themselves a cigarette, a movie, or an hour of television—or perhaps something even more interesting!—when they complete a given piece of work. There is nothing wrong with such rewards as long as their use is only a game played to whet interest, but matters can go too far. A degree, diploma, or certificate, for example, is a respected evidence that a man or woman has achieved a certain level or kind of education, but it is the learning that counts, not the piece of paper. Whenever an adult reverses those values and seeks not to learn but to have only the evidence of learning, he begins to destroy his ability to gain the greater satisfaction which comes from the development of his own potentialities.

3. REMEMBER THE STRENGTH OF YOUR OWN POINT OF VIEW

Your learning is strongly influenced by the point of view you bring to it. Jerome Bruner and Cecile Goodman [2] have shown this to be true in a striking experiment. They cut out gray disks of paper the size of a penny, a nickel, a dime, a quarter, and a fifty-cent piece and asked children to draw circles of the same size. These circles usually did not vary more than 5 per cent from the correct size. Then the investigators used actual coins and gave the same instructions. At once the children's estimates of the size increased. The circles were at least 15 per cent larger than the coins. The more valuable the coins, generally speaking, the more the children overestimated the size. For example, they saw the quarter as being more than 35 per cent larger than it actually was.

An even more striking next step was then taken. The same experiment was carried out with a group of children from wealthy homes and a group of children from poor homes. The wealthy children overestimated the size of the coins from 10 to 20 per cent. The poor children overestimated from 20 to 50 per cent. In both cases, the overestimation of size tended to increase with the value of the coin.

The results of this study seem to show that if an object has no value to a person, he can make fairly good estimates of it, but if it does have value, he sees it as being larger than it is. And the higher the value, the more he will overestimate its importance.

The experiences of all adults have brought them, consciously or not, to many conclusions about what is good and what is bad. Therefore, as mature men and women approach an educational activity, they may lack a proper sense of proportion and a desirable balance of judgment. A labor leader will emphasize some aspects of economics and an industrialist will emphasize others, not necessarily because either really chooses to do so. They simply cannot help their biased viewpoints.

Therefore, as you study, keep in mind the strength of your own point of view. As you make estimates and judgments, be aware that you may be seeing things not in a proper balance and proportion but distorted by the values you have acquired. When bias stands in your way, it is time to change directions.

Turning the matter around, treat the varying points of view of others as a positive value in your pattern of learning. Part of the endless enjoyment of classes and groups is the discovery and rediscovery of the fascinating differences among people. It is rewarding, too, constantly to ask oneself why each individual holds the views he does and what has made him become the kind of person he is.

Most important of all, do not let your established values harden into such fixed beliefs that you cannot tolerate new ideas. When this happens, the process of education ceases. A discussion group may intensely dislike a book which it is asked to read, but if the members can open their minds to it, seek to understand what the author was trying to do and why, and discuss their views as to his success, their understanding will be enlarged. Often they will end up still disliking the book—but out of knowledge, not out of ignorance.

4. ACTIVELY FIT NEW IDEAS AND NEW FACTS INTO CONTEXT

Your greatest asset as an adult learner is the fact that your experience enables you to see relationships. When a new idea or fact is presented, you can understand it because you have background and perspective. And you can remember it because you can associate it with what you already know and therefore give it meaning. If you doubt this fact, try reading again some substantial work which you first read as a child, perhaps *Ivanhoe, Julius Caesar,* or *David Copperfield.* How that book has changed!

Here is firsthand evidence from two adult students on this point:

Picking up study again, I find my age (about forty-nine) offers some advantages to education over the younger ages. This is especially so since my field of interest is in business administration. I find that my years and variety of experiences in business are a great help to me in understanding and grasping the basic principles. I really sympathize with young people who are so short on any experience that could be of help.

To find a technique of study during college was my entire problem in getting through. When I started back in to study again, after some time in the business world, I found I had unknowingly developed the technique of association. I was able to see examples of my course in everyday business working.

The fund of experience of adults is built up gradually and constantly throughout their lives. Everybody, for example, accumulates a set of keys—to the front door, to the car, to the locker or the office door at work, to the tool shed, to the fishing box, to the sewing machine, to suitcases, and to all the other things and places which we think should be kept locked. As each new key comes along, the man who receives it looks at it, establishes its general shape, tries it (incidentally learning at that point whether its flat side should be up or down), and puts it on his key ring. With no ado, his knowledge has been increased and his future behavior changed.

Now think about a man who has grown up in a primitive-tribe society where everything is shared and nothing is private. Consider what he would confront if he went to a city to work. Among the baffling and confusing things that he would before long have to confront would be his first lock and key. We can imagine how complicated they would seem to him, and he would very likely marvel at their strangeness. Soon he would need a second lock and key. Since they were different in design, he might not relate them to his first set. After a while, however, he would gradually come to understand the general idea of locks and keys. And then, perhaps much later, he would reflect about the differences between his village where all good things are shared and his new life where they seem to be jealously guarded.

The same basic situation would occur if an American went to live in a tribal village. To survive, he would need to build a new set of associations and skills. It might be a long time before he adopted all the general practices of the village and even longer before he could understand how the basic ideas and values of the villagers affected what they did.

The ability to learn most easily the information for which a foundation has been laid is illustrated every day in the lives of everyone. How do you read the newspaper? You may say that you read it from cover to cover, but if you were given an examination over what you had read on any given day, great gaps in your reading might be revealed. You have a good understanding of what is going on at city hall, so you read carefully all the stories that have to do with local government—and remember what you read. Since you know nothing about high society, you hastily turn over the pages which have to do with its affairs. Somebody else, with opposite interests and knowledge, would reverse your pattern of reading.

Information also helps to build an understanding of principles. For example, earlier in this chapter, the names of Heifetz, Tolstoy, Aristotle, and Spinoza were used. Did they mean anything to you? If so, you got the point which was being made, and you probably remember it. If not, the names did nothing to help you.

One way to build your understanding, therefore, is always to look for associations between the new matter to be learned and what you already know. This process occurs naturally enough to make most learning experiences immediately significant. When it doesn't, you should deliberately seek to find parallels or to make applications. As one man put it:

> When a subject is being taught in a general fashion, the individual will more quickly grasp the details if he applies his new-found knowledge to a specific problem in his own life. The student then is not only working in familiar ground, where mistakes will be obvious to him, but by seeing an immediate application he is encouraged in his studies.

If a field is completely new to you, the wisest course of action is to spend some time trying to get at the fundamentals so that you have a solid basis on which to build. Suppose, for example, you feel you ought to know more about international affairs. The newspapers, the magazines, television, and radio bring floods of information about it—but this information is presented by people who are knowledgeable in the field and is understood best by those who have a similar knowledge. It is taken for granted that you will know the meaning of "balance of power," "sovereignty," the Atlantic Alliance, UNESCO, and other such terms. Suppose you don't! In that case, the meaning is lost to you.

If you want to become knowledgeable about world affairs, you have two major courses of action. One is to go on painfully and laboriously reading about current events, clearing up various terms as you proceed, but, for the most part, accepting new ideas on faith and getting only a crude sense of what is being said, thereby missing the finer shades of meaning. The alternative action (and the more sensible) is to take a course, read a textbook, or in some other fashion get a basic introduction to the subject. When you have laid the groundwork, then all your later reading and viewing will have a deeper meaning than they did before.

You may find it wise deliberately to broaden the base of your knowledge without regard for any immediate purpose. You have learned many things in the past which later on proved to be useful in ways that you did not anticipate when you learned them. If you set your mind to acquiring totally new areas of knowledge, you will usually find in the future that they have values you do not now contemplate. A powerful businessman followed this practice consistently:

> This is a complicated company that I'm head of, and you see relationships everywhere. Of course, I have to stay on top of the new ideas in the field of business and management. But that isn't enough. That's expected of everybody. If I have been able to move out in front, it's because I've deliberately tried to study all kinds of strange things—like modern art or Renaissance painting or the history of ancient Greece or the geography of Africa. You'd be surprised how often these off-beat subjects turn up some new idea or relationship that is really useful to me. And of course I get a great kick out of being able to make associations all over the place and really understanding what all kinds of people are talking about—not just pretending that I do!

Underlying these suggestions is the fact that you must constantly be active in your learning. Chapter 5 includes a number of techniques for doing so, but meanwhile here is how four successful students follow this principle:

> I don't accept blindly those statements contained in a text. I ask instead, consciously or not, "What is he trying to say? Is the reasoning good? How does this relate with what has gone before?" As a

consequence, the text seems less dry, more interesting, and less like a monologue.

To make the subject more interesting I try to create a broad background of interest. I am studying Spanish. I have read about the history of Mexico—traditions, music, great artists, and so on.

Knowledge is only retained in response to your own mental process of trying to find an answer. In other words, I can "memorize" the fact that Columbus discovered America in 1492, but if memorized only once, this information will gradually be lost. However, if I have really and earnestly asked and wondered in what year Columbus discovered America and have then found out that it was 1492, I will probably never forget it.

Don't just read the assignment. Instead, practice doing what you'll be called on to do later. Write things out, explain the laws, work the problems, apply the formulas. Don't try to learn to swim in an armchair.

This last remark is a fine piece of advice that deserves repeating. Don't try to learn to swim in an armchair!

5. SEEK HELP AND SUPPORT WHEN YOU NEED IT

Sometimes an adult will choose to learn by himself, and sometimes he will choose to learn with others. A balanced learning program combines many elements, though not all at the same time. But while adults often teach themselves what they want to know, they may run into real dangers if they rely on this method too consistently. John Stuart Mill [3], the great English economist, put the matter very well when he said, "a clever self-educated man . . . often sees what men trained in routine do not see, but falls into errors for want of knowing things which have long been known . . . he has acquired much of the pre-existing knowledge, or he could not have got on at all; but what he knows of it he has picked up in fragments and at random. . . ."

One time when it is well to seek out a teacher is when you are beginning the study of a new subject. You would not start on an automobile trip without a road map, and you should not begin a journey into an unexplored area of knowledge without the best guidance you can get. (Remember Route 25.)

A second time when you need help is when you bog down in your studies. At this point, many people simply stop. They would be wise instead to find someone who understands their particular difficulties. Sometimes this person may be a teacher, sometimes a friend. Sometimes it may be a counselor who can use special techniques to make an appraisal of your abilities and capacities. Other people can help you over difficult places in your study and, even more fundamentally, can assist you to make a realistic judgment about your ability, your knowledge, and your interest.

A third time when it is wise to seek help is when you feel the need of the social stimulation of a class or a group. Sometimes it is wise to turn to reading and independent study as a way of finding quietness and tranquility in the midst of a busy life. At such a time, solitude is the prize. But everybody also needs the sparkle and interest of a shared experience, and the support which comes from realizing that many people share the same interests and problems. As Henry Van Dyke [4] once wrote, "Knowledge may be gained from books; but the love of knowledge is transmitted only by personal contact."

The help and reinforcement of other students may come outside of class as well as in it. One woman said:

I immediately continue discussions with one of my classmates on the way home, if possible, and always with my husband when I get home. This gives me other people's ideas and impresses the whole thing on my mind so there is less need for later review.

It is very important to have family support and encouragement for any sustained learning program. This point is made very well by a husband and by a mother:

My wife felt left out and thus enrolled in the basic humanities course. She had been out of school for a long time, and it was not easy for her to adapt to study habits so I taught her to read straight through the *Republic* and then go back and reread again for the essence of the work. It worked too damn well. Now I find I have to define Socrates. So much for higher education.

My children seem to be quite interested in the fact that Mommy goes to school, too. I think perhaps this has increased their respect for the learning process. They often ask how I did on a quiz and, of course, are very aware of annual examination time.

Still another student recommends "exchanging telephone numbers so that students may exchange ideas and data." Perhaps it should be noted, however, that he is a twenty-seven-year-old bachelor.

6. LEARN BEYOND THE POINT NECESSARY FOR IMMEDIATE RECALL

We all learn many things we do not really wish to remember—and which we promptly forget. For example, if you are going to call on somebody at an unfamiliar location, you will probably repeat the address several times and remember it until it has served its purpose. Then you will very likely let it slip from your thoughts and your memory. If you go back to the same address again, you will be guided chiefly by your recollection of the appearance of the street and the building.

If you want to remember something permanently, however, you must do what the psychologist calls *over-learning*. Even after you can recall the fact or perform the skill perfectly, you should keep on reviewing it. A day later, review it again. Keep repeating this habit until there is no danger that it can slip from your memory. It may seem wasteful to follow this practice when you could be using your time to better advantage going on to something new. Such is not the case. By overlearning you reinforce the gains you have already made. As one man put it:

> It is the extra 10 per cent that makes a good student. A baseball player hits .260 and we say "lousy hitter." Another hits .300, "good hitter." The difference is four more hits in every 100 times at bat. As a student, go after four more hits.

7. USE PSYCHOLOGICAL AS WELL AS LOGICAL PRACTICES

You have already had an illustration of this rule. In Chapter 1 you were urged first to skim this book, then to read it, and then to examine it closely. Now it seems illogical to many people not to go through a book thoroughly, digesting a paragraph at a time. Yet research has shown that the way here recommended is better.

The psychological and the logical are not really opposed to one another. When we use a "psychological" approach, we are simply realizing a deeper and more inward kind of logic which applies to what we do. Wisdom comes in knowing that you should sometimes use this deeper logic. Many a scientific investigator has tried again and again to work his way out of a difficulty, using all his resources of knowledge and technique, only to fail each time. But sometime later, when he had ceased thinking about the problem, the clue to its answer suddenly flashed into his mind.

Many psychological methods of approach are suggested throughout this book, and every student will develop his own. Here are a few reported by three successful adult students:

> I do the easy jobs first, the ones I understand. This gives me confidence with the more difficult problems.

> Sometimes I put ideas on paper, or in my mental refrigerator, and let them jell before accepting them. It is good to sleep on ideas. Their absurdity or basic soundness often becomes more pertinent in the next day's cold, clear dawn of reason.

> I'm a great believer in the second wind, so when I hit a snag, I pour another cup of coffee. On a bad snag, I start a game of solitaire. I'm not sure of the psychology of this, but I presume my subconscious mind continues to operate while my conscious mind is taking a breather. I never out-and-out quit working if I get bogged down, or I'd never get this second wind.

Psychological approaches alone are never sufficient. The scientific investigator cannot merely sit around waiting for the answer to come without first stocking his mind with all of the basic factors of which it is composed. And the man or woman who wants to learn must remember that nothing worth knowing can be gained without effort.

SEVEN PRINCIPLES AND
THREE READINGS

These, then, are seven principles which should guide those who wish to learn. They are basic to the more specific advice given in the later chapters of this book.

If you are doing your first skimming, you may not remember any of the principles very distinctly at this point. It doesn't really matter for (if you like the book) you will be passing this way again.

If you are on your second reading, you should be able to remember most of the principles. Try to do so. Then go back through the chapter and put a check mark by the ones you didn't remember. Try once again to recall all seven. The particular words don't matter; it is the ideas that count. Keep on until you have overlearned all seven.

If you are on your third reading, you may want to reflect thoughtfully about your own performance on each of the seven. Or you may want to discover the ways in which they are basic to many of the more detailed suggestions on later pages. If you know them well now, sometime in the future, when you happen to be stuck in your learning endeavors, you may find that one of the seven is the key which will unlock your difficulty.

Chapter 4

The Time, the Place, and the Strategy

The distinguished gray-haired man leaned back, took off his heavy-rimmed glasses, and looked with level eyes across his mahogany desk. "So you're writing a book on how to learn," he said. "Well, so far as I'm concerned, learning was no great achievement. I knew what I wanted and how to get it. You've got to prepare yourself to take advantage of the opportunities that come along. Everyone gets twenty-four hours a day to devote to whatever he wants to do. One or two old acquaintances have envied me for what I have achieved. They could have done the same. All they had to do was devote a part of *their* twenty-four hours to study rather than to something else."

His advice was echoed in various ways by many of the 470 successful adult students consulted in writing this book. Again and again, they made the same basic point: *If you want to do any serious and continued study, be sure to allow time for it, and use that time in the right way.*

LEARNING AND YOUR TOTAL SCHEDULE

Many people feel that they can add the new activity of study to everything they are already doing. They persuade themselves that it will not take much time to learn to speak Italian, to study the plays of Shakespeare, to master advanced electronics, or to understand the workings of the United Nations. They fail to realize that if they are going to take a course on Tuesday nights, they cannot do what they usually do on those evenings and that they must also plan extra time to study both before and after the class meeting. Something has to be crowded out.

Adults must fit their study into the complicated patterns of their busy days. The housewife, the welder, the secretary, the union official, the traveling salesman, the executive, the clerk in a store, the theater usher, the farmer, the waitress—each has a distinctive rhythm of life established by the work he does. This variation among people is made even greater by the places they live, the amount of money they have, the size of their families, the extent of their travel, and the many other ways each person differs from every other.

Then, too, adults use many different learning techniques, each of which has its special time requirements. Men and women may take classes or study entirely by themselves. They may watch a television course or enroll in a correspondence school, go systematically on nature walks or join a discussion group, go to a university for a conference, or do any of the countless other things available.

But everybody, when he decides to settle down to serious study, discovers that he must first find a time and a place for it and then learn how to use both to best advantage. Here is how four successful students make this point:

> You have to take a look at what you are doing and make choices.

> Don't enroll unless you are fully prepared to give up the necessary amount of free time during the week.

Being a single man, I was very fond of the "bright lights." Between work, school, and having a good time, one of them was going lacking, which was studying. I decided one of them had to go. So it was "bright lights." I had to reorganize my time so I could do justice to my studies and still have a little recreation, with happy results.

After approximately three weeks of forbidding myself social activities and forcing myself to study, I managed to develop the habit once again and subsequently resumed my social activities.

A REGULAR PATTERN OF LEARNING

People who say that they never have enough time to do what they want are like people who complain that they do not have enough money to buy all the things they would like to have. In most families money is limited, but those who take careful stock of what they own and plan their spending wisely get a lot more than do those who simply go along from day to day, buying on impulse and feeling abused because they never have enough cash. The demands on some people's time may be so great that they do not have any margin left. The only way to find out if that is true is to examine one's total pattern of living and see whether any time can be used for study.

Most people find it essential to establish a regular schedule for learning. Time must be set aside for the purpose, just as money is budgeted to pay for rent, food, or doctor's bills. Sometimes this process is fairly simple. One man, for example, used this procedure: "Knowing my previous responsibilities for the rest of the week, I set aside the night after the class and the night before the class. This gave me an opportunity to go over what we had already studied and the teacher's ideas on the subject while it was fresh in my mind and to study for the next assignment." Other people like to plan their time in great detail, allotting every hour to some purpose. But whether the scheduling is simple or complicated, some kind of plan should be made and followed. Here are some suggestions about how to do so.

1. If you are just starting on an organized learning program, do not be too ambitious. Many men and women suddenly have a feeling of revulsion against the way they have been wasting their time. They think they can make up immediately for many lost years by beginning a heroic program of study. Almost always, the result is bad. They cannot carry the new load and before long they give up the whole enterprise and relapse into their former ways. It is wiser to build up an involvement in educative activities gradually, never taking on more than can be accomplished. In the lives of most adults, study cannot become an all-absorbing passion. It is not sensible to act as if it could.

2. Do not assume that you can increase your capacity to learn merely by adding more and more hours of study. Of course you need to allow the right amount —and it will vary from person to person—but proper use of the time must also be taken into account. Studying university students, E. G. Williamson [1] found that

> . . . a minimum of eighteen to twenty hours and a maximum of thirty to thirty-five hours of study a week should permit students to get the grades that their academic aptitude makes possible. Within these limits, improvement in study skills, reading habits, and interest and pride in studying

for the sake of being well trained professionally are the important factors to note in any attempt to improve the scholarship of students.

Several investigations have shown that, with few exceptions, the university students who get the highest grades are those who also excel in other activities. The well-balanced student does not concentrate solely on his books. He leaves ample time for other things—*but he uses his study time to fullest advantage.*

3. If you decide to make a comprehensive schedule covering all your activities, use this basic technique.

Draw up a chart with a column for each day of the week. Draw lines across the chart marking different intervals of the day. You may want to do so on an hour-by-hour basis, or you may want merely to mark out such large blocks of time as "morning," "afternoon," and "evening." (It will be useful, by the way, to make several copies of this chart. You will need one or two for practice before you achieve the right combination.)

On a separate sheet of paper, make a list of your regular and recurrent activities and the amount of time needed by each. Be realistic about the estimates of time. Include, for example, not merely the number of hours you are on the job, but also the time you need to get to and from work. Think of everything you must do or want to do: sleep, meals, church, reading newspapers and magazines, meetings, recreation, dressing and undressing, housekeeping, care of your person and your clothes, and anything else which takes substantial time. Allow some margin of time for activities you haven't thought of or for the special events or crises which occur in everyone's life.

On your weekly chart, block in your activities, beginning with those which are fixed, such as church, work, and sleep. See what major blocks of time are left. Assign as many of them to learning as you think feasible and wise. Allow an extra margin of time for emergencies. (Although you may plan to read every Tuesday night, on some Tuesdays people will visit or there will be a special program on television you want very much to see. During that week, shift your reading to one of the alternate times.) Then fill in the schedule with other activities, leaving as much flexibility and as many comfortable margins as you can.

4. Study at the time most suitable to you. People vary greatly in the hours of the day when they do their best work. Here, for example, are opposing points of view:

> I have found that an hour of study in the morning before leaving for work is worth two hours in the evening. My mind seems more receptive to study before it is cluttered with problems at the office. As I drive to work, I can think of what I have read and digest it.

> I don't like to try to learn anything until late in the evening. By then I can have had a leisurely dinner and the problems of the day have gotten unwound. Then, too, it is quiet. It isn't until the late evening hours that I really come alive.

Some people like to study just after they wake up; others, just before they go to sleep. Some people like to study just before they have exercise, recreation, or a meal; others, just after. Try to find out when you do your best learning, experimenting with various times. Then concentrate your efforts to take advantage of what you have discovered about yourself.

5. Space your learning periods during the week rather than concentrating them all at one time. This practice will help you avoid fatigue and give you several fresh approaches rather than just one. It will also keep

your mind actively at work in between the sessions. You will find yourself reflecting again and again about the material you are learning.

6. If you are studying several different subjects, do not spend too long on each one at any given learning period. If you are taking two courses, for example, divide your study time in half, so that you can cover both subjects. This practice gives you some of the advantages of spaced learning. It also provides for variety of approach and helps establish the relationships between one subject and another.

7. Plan in advance for peak periods of study. If you were making a family budget, you would realize that there are certain expenditures, such as a new car or a family vacation, which do not come every week or month; you must think about them in advance to have enough money when the time comes. In many study programs, there are similar peaks of effort—examinations, term-paper writing time, or other similar requirements. Be sure to take account of this fact in your time schedule.

8. Post your schedule in a prominent place and begin to follow it at once. If you develop a formal week-long schedule, put it into effect immediately. If you merely plan to devote a certain time to study, do so at the next opportunity. The basic way to establish a new habit is to begin practicing it. The longer you delay, the less likely you are to be able to succeed.

9. Revise your schedule if it seems wise to do so. Your first plan will almost certainly not be the best one. You may have forgotten some of the things you need to do. You may discover that you need more or less time to learn than you allowed. You may realize that a different pattern of work, study, and play would permit you to do all three more efficiently than your first plan. If you do decide to change your schedule, do so at once. Begin to practice the new habit.

10. Once you have worked out the best schedule for yourself, follow it as rigorously as you can. If you have decided to start studying mathematics on your teaching machine at eight o'clock, do so without fail. You need the support of a habit, and you cannot get that support without careful practice.

11. Let everybody know about your plans. Most people will be considerate enough to keep from interrupting you. If you have resolved to work on a correspondence course from ten to twelve each weekday morning (after the house is spruced up and before the children come home for lunch), your friends will soon learn to call you before or after that time. Then, too, if you announce your plans, you won't want to admit later on that you haven't followed them!

Not everybody is willing to set up so formal a pattern as the one suggested here—and many people lead such necessarily varied lives that no exact schedule is realistic. But careful planning usually pays off here as elsewhere in life. In this case, its reward is a greatly increased capacity to find time to do what you'd like.

USING STRATEGY IN YOUR TIMING

When you have established a schedule of periods of study, you have taken a first and essential step. You must next think about combining those periods into a meaningful sequence so that each reinforces the others. The most intelligent way to do so is to organize them in terms of your learning plan.

You may be taking a course either in a class or by correspondence. You may be studying a major book or a group of books. Or you may be trying to understand the life, literature, and history of a foreign country. Whether your plan is one of these or any other, you must use strategy in the timing of your study. For the sake of simplicity, a course taken in class is used here as an illustration, but the principles suggested apply to any other learning program.

1. At your first study session, get an overall view of the purposes and content of the whole course. Go through the course outline. If there is a text, skim through it, reading the introduction and looking at the headings of the chapters and the major sections. Think about the teacher and his particular approach to the subject. Review the timing of the course—how many sessions there will be, when examinations are scheduled, and what other requirements have been set.

2. At each subsequent study session, take a little time to reflect how the particular topic you are working on relates to the whole course.

3. As soon after each class period as possible, schedule a study period to review what you learned in class. H. A. Peterson and his associates [2] have shown that review is particularly effective at two times, one near the period of learning, the other just before the examination. Most people know that the latter is true but are not aware that they can greatly increase their retention of material if they go over it soon after they have first learned it.

4. At this same study period, begin your preparation for the next class or the next assignment. Get it broadly in mind so that you can reflect about it and lay a foundation for more detailed study.

5. Schedule another study period before the next class. Once again review what you learned. This time, however, concentrate on what you need to know when you go to class so that you will be prepared for recita-

tion or discussion and will have a suitable background for the lecture or other presentation that the instructor makes.

6. When given an assignment, complete it as soon as possible after class. Then, if there is time, go over it again before you hand it in, making any changes which second thought indicates are advisable. One adult student had this idea when he said:

> I have found that a whole weekend can be wasted because an important assignment is postponed from now to this afternoon to this evening to tomorrow and so on, when it could have been completed Friday evening and would therefore be off the mind during the weekend. In my case, at least, I find there is a tendency to allow an uncompleted assignment to affect the other things I do, decreasing my efficiency all around.

7. If you find you have a bit of extra time at your study sessions, go back to review earlier lessons, particularly those which you are not sure you can adequately recall. Remember the importance of overlearning.

8. As you draw toward the end of a course, take particular pains to examine its whole pattern. Put your knowledge (which is now much deeper than it was earlier) into the necessary perspective. If you need to memorize facts, fit them into some context.

If this specific strategy in the timing of the study does not apply in your case, plan one which does, using the same general principles. Learning is most significant when it involves the mastery of ideas, concepts, and subject matter too complex or too large to be fully comprehended in a single learning period. Therefore, the periods available must be organized in such a way as to make the desired mastery possible.

USING EACH STUDY PERIOD
MOST EFFECTIVELY

When the 470 adults consulted in the preparation of this book were asked to name the chief problem they encountered in their efforts to learn, a large number (88) said that they had had trouble learning to concentrate. Others put the same matter in different ways: difficulty in directing thought (51); too many distractions (4); fatigue or exhaustion (29); difficulty in studying (25); and a tendency to procrastinate (14). All these problems are basically the same. When trying to learn, many people find they can't hold their minds on what they want to do. For example:

> Having to deal with several things simultaneously and constantly in business and in the home the last few years, I am finding it extremely difficult to focus my attention on one thing and keep it there. My mind keeps racing off to other problems, schedules, and plans.

> As the mother of three small children, I find I've become so used to listening for them, to their conversations, etc., that concentration has become rather difficult. I'm now trying to shut out these noises I've spent several years training myself to hear automatically.

The secret of concentration is to become as actively engaged as possible in the task at hand. Suppose one of the children has developed a cough. You worry about him and wonder if he will be able to go to school tomorrow. If he isn't, your plans for a trip downtown shopping may have to be changed, and you'll need to call Betty to bow out of the lunch she's having. You know you really can't decide anything until morning.

Still, it's worrisome. If you sit down to read at your scheduled study hour, you find that the problem steals back into your mind again and again. You simply cannot hold your attention on what you know you should be doing. But if you have a pencil and paper at hand and make an outline while you read, you may find that just that little bit of activity itself will help keep your mind focused on what you want to do.

This need to interact constantly with the material at hand is so important that it is the subject of the next chapter. In a sense, that chapter really gives the essential advice on how to concentrate. But there are also a number of techniques or practices you may find useful in helping you take the fullest advantage of each study period.

1. Be sure you have all of your needed study materials available before you start. An accomplished "time waster" can kill an entire evening by neglecting this suggestion. He sits down with his book. Then he remembers he needs a pencil and paper. He can't find the paper and has to ask his wife where it is, in the process delivering himself of a few remarks about tidy housekeeping, to which she does not hesitate to respond. Then the pencil needs sharpening, and as he goes to the sharpener, he passes by the telephone which reminds him that he should call Joe to fix up a golf date. Back at the desk, he presently comes on a word he doesn't know. He goes to the dictionary, but while getting it from the shelf, notices a book of poetry he used in college. Pulling it down, he browses reminiscently through its pages. Finally carrying the dictionary back to his desk, he realizes he is hungry and goes to the icebox, where he is promptly joined by his son, Bob, who wants to talk about the forthcoming heavyweight fight. After a stimulating discussion, he goes back to his desk and settles in—with book, pencil, paper, and dictionary. He starts over because he has forgotten the organization of the chapter. Presently he grows sleepy and discovers

it is almost time for the ten o'clock news. At ten-fifteen he rejoins his wife, remarking that he has put in a really good evening of study!

2. Set up facilitating rather than time-wasting rituals. Many baseball pitchers go through an elaborate routine before every throw. One major league player, for example, invariably dries his hands, hitches up his pants, pulls down his cap, lifts each of his feet in turn, wets his lips, touches the ball to his right hip—and then gets in position for the pitch. Few adults are immune from this same kind of superstitious behavior. For some people a whole series of ceremonies is essential. Everything must be just so—the right clothes, the right placement of the chair, the right position of the light, the door closed, and every separate member of the family admonished to maintain a deathly hush. Such pre-study rituals may be looked upon with an indulgent eye as long as they do not get in the way of study itself. But, if possible, one should try to set up procedures which aid study, not which prevent it. As was just suggested, have all materials available from the start. Set up the desk, chair, and other aspects of the study situation *before* the time of beginning. Begin promptly. Since we all have rituals, the more supportive they are, the better.

3. If you are tired, find a time when you can study with a fresher outlook. Fatigue is the greatest enemy of concentration. Perhaps there is an alternate time you can use. Perhaps your whole schedule needs reexamination. Approach the matter of your own tiredness positively, realizing that rest will make everything look brighter. Do not force yourself too hard, or you will begin to build up negative rather than positive associations.

4. Arrange matters so that you will have as few distractions as possible. You should think about this principle when you make your basic schedule, setting a time for learning which is as free of interruption as you can

make it. In a busy household, it is hard to block out all distraction—but do what you can. If somebody telephones, the person who answers can say that you'll call back later. If a friend drops in, let your wife do the entertaining until you finish what you are doing. Most people will understand your need to concentrate—and will help you if they realize its importance to you.

5. Confront the fact that the chief handicap provided by distractions is your emotional response to them. If somebody starts singing in the next room, it usually isn't the noise that bothers you. It is the fact that he could be so inconsiderate! If somebody comes to call and you hear the sound of laughter in the living room, you are bothered chiefly by the feeling that you are being left out of a pleasant social occasion and that maybe people will think you odd for keeping your nose in a book. If somebody telephones to invite you to go on a picnic, it is not the three-minute call which is destructive. It is the half-hour reverie about the coming social occasion. If you gain this insight into your reactions, you will be helped to attack the problem of interruptions at its true source: within your own feelings and emotions.

6. When you start to study, begin with something you know you can do easily. The assurance you gain will help you take on more difficult tasks.

7. Start with relatively brief sessions of study and gradually extend their length. (At every session, however, allow time to complete some meaningful whole. Don't stop halfway through a page or with only a part of the total skill you are practicing.) When an athlete gets in condition for a match, he builds up his practice periods gradually as he gains mastery over his muscles. You should do the same. Study until you find your attention wandering almost uncontrollably. Stop for a while. Then start again. Before long, your periods of successful concentration will lengthen appreciably.

8. Take rest periods in which you do something different. A good general rule, when you are well back into the practice of learning, might be to concentrate for fifty minutes and then take a ten-minute break. During this time, do something actively different from your study. Don't just prowl around the house waiting for the ten minutes to be up. At the end of the ten minutes, be sure to go back to work again.

9. Before taking a break, know exactly what you will do when you resume study. After even a brief pause, you need to help yourself get started again.

10. If you keep being distracted by thinking of other things to do, make a note of them. One of the reasons they stay on your mind is your fear of forgetting them. By jotting down a note to remind yourself to do them later, you allay that fear and keep your concentration.

11. If you have a problem which just won't go out of your mind, confront it directly, analyze it, think about possible solutions, and write them down. Decide that if Jimmy can't go to school tomorrow, you will have to (a) see if Mrs. Jenkins can take care of him, or (b) postpone your shopping and call Betty. Analyzing a problem in this way reduces its importance and enables you to get it off your mind.

12. Review your incentives and try to rekindle your enthusiasm for your study goals. When you first had the idea of learning to typewrite, you thought it would be wonderful to have a skill you could use in so many ways in your daily life and which would be a way to earn money if you ever had to do so. Sometimes, though, when you are slogging along at twelve words a minute and haven't noticed improvement for quite a while, you may need to give yourself a pep talk to call back your earlier enthusiasm and to reassure yourself that your original purposes are still as important as they ever were.

13. Set up an immediate reward for good perform-

ance. Tell yourself that if you really concentrate during this last fifty minutes of study, you'll fix yourself a milk shake, start that new thriller you bought, or drop over next door to see the Summersbys.

14. If your difficulties in concentrating continue despite anything you can do, seek special counsel or training. Perhaps you have a medical problem, such as poor eyesight or an inadequate diet. Perhaps you need special guidance from a teacher, who can help you surmount difficulties you don't realize you have. Perhaps you need a course in study skills or remedial reading. Perhaps you need to talk out your basic problems with a counselor.

CHOOSING THE BEST PLACE TO STUDY

As has been suggested throughout this chapter, the time and the place of learning are closely related.

People *can* learn under almost any conditions. For example, consider a matter as basic as the amount of light available. In a comprehensive review of the evidence, F. C. Rose and S. M. Rostas [3] concluded that "given sufficient light to distinguish print . . . and freedom to read the material at the preferred distance from the eyes, almost any factor other than illumination seems to play a more important role in reading efficiency than illumination." Adults are astonishingly adaptable and, if they want to do so, can surmount all kinds of inadequacies and distractions. If you cannot find "the right place to work," therefore, you should not abandon your efforts to learn.

Generally speaking, however, it is wise to find the best place possible in which to do your studying. The ideal is to have your own den or study, which can be kept constantly ready for your use, with everything you need conveniently arranged. Alternatively, you may be able to set aside one part of a room, as isolated as possible from distracting influences. If a separate study area can't be managed, you will need to find the most convenient location with a working space which you can set up and dismantle each time you study. If none of these arrangements can be made, you may have to look outside your home and consider using the reading room of the public library or some other similar place.

You will want to find a location where the basic conditions for work are as good as possible and where distractions are at a minimum. The most important principle is to select a spot where you can build up a continuing association with study—where the location does not mean anything other than the place where you learn. When you sit down at the desk, you automatically go to work.

In choosing the right place, there are several things to consider.

1. The place you choose should be as quiet as possible. Unless you feel very strongly that you *must* have music to help you study or to drown out distracting noises, do not have it. Henderson, Crews, and Barlow [4] have shown that music is often a disturbing influence while studying, even for those who are used to keeping the radio or record player on.

2. If you are studying by yourself, it is usually best if you can be alone in the room. If you are studying with someone else or with a group, nonparticipants should not be present.

3. Your chair should be comfortable but not relaxing.

4. If you use a desk, choose one which is conducive to good posture and which has a large top surface and adequate storage space.

5. Have within your vision only a blank wall and those objects necessary for study. (Somerset Maugham built a study with a magnificent view of the Mediter-

ranean—but he could write nothing until he had the window bricked up.) Any irrelevant objects are likely to cause your mind to wander. If you study at the library, choose a seat which offers you the most isolated and restricted view possible.

6. Keep your study space neat and tidy.

7. Keep the room at the most comfortable temperature you can manage and allow for suitable ventilation.

8. Be sure that the lighting is adequate and comfortable for you, neither too dim nor too bright. Never let the light shine directly into your eyes. There should not be a great difference between the light which is shining directly on your work and the general illumination in the room.

Other factors need to be considered when you are learning in some special way, such as drawing or painting, watching a television course, or listening to tapes on your recorder. Remember, however, that all the elements you take into account in choosing the right space are merely guides. Do not let the absence of any of them become a barrier to your progress.

FITTING LEARNING INTO THE ROUTINES OF LIFE

The great athlete was walking down the street. Those behind him could see his powerful shoulders writhing under his coat as his clenched fists turned from side to side. A friend, catching up, asked, "Jack, is anything wrong?" Jack looked sheepish. "Naw," he answered, "I was just exercising."

Many adult students would think that Jack was using a good principle. They have found that although they schedule regular times and places for study as he did for exercise, they can supplement their learning by taking advantage of spare moments or by using the ordinary affairs of life to deepen or to broaden their education. This principle can be put into effect in various ways.

1. Some people take advantage of the many spare moments of life to read or review the materials they study. They record a television lesson on the tape recorder and play it back while ironing or shining shoes. They keep a book in their pocket or purse to read during otherwise idle moments—on an airplane, a train, or a bus; while standing in lines or sitting at the doctor's office; and when waiting for people to arrive to keep their appointments. As one woman put it:

> As a housewife I have had to utilize every moment possible to study: (1) While washing dishes, I prop the study book on the soap dish. (2) While waiting for an answer to a telephone call, I keep the book close at hand. (3) Before going to sleep at night, I read a problem in the course of study, and often mentally digest it by morning. (4) My book goes with me everywhere, for there are always moments of waiting during which studying may be done. (5) Except for illness, I do daily studying. (6) I try to eliminate trivia from my mental meanderings.

2. Other people plan special aids to use in spare moments. They keep a notebook and pencil handy to jot down ideas or to draft paragraphs for a report they are writing. If they are trying to memorize something, they prepare special memory aids. Anyone trying to learn a foreign vocabulary, for example, might make a set of cards, each of which has a foreign word on one side and its English translation on the other.

3. Sometimes it is awkward or inconvenient to use a book or a special memory aid. Under such circumstances, many adults use spare moments to reflect about whatever they happen to be learning. As one woman

said, "When I can't read, I think, turning over in my mind the last chapter I read or the latest classroom discussion. I do this while doing dishes, laundry, ironing, or whatever." Still another woman said, "This same principle can be applied whether you're waiting for the dentist or getting your hair done."

4. More informally, one can try to increase one's powers of observation. Most people have read about Sherlock Holmes's ability to observe a great deal about a stranger. While nobody ever approaches the great master in this respect, it is possible to learn a lot by observation. Knowledge of human character is heightened by an effort to understand why people behave as they do. The comprehension of political or social principles is made deeper by relating news events or special happenings to some underlying pattern of causation. The appreciation of art and of music may be made greater by paying close attention to any art objects or music one may experience.

5. Finally, one can practice the social skills which are so much a part of all meaningful learning. Idle chatter and small talk is a normal part of life and a useful way of getting along smoothly and easily, but sometimes it can be elevated into a real conversation, rewarding to all concerned. An argument may be subtly shaped into a discussion. A tendency to be opinionated can be diminished by the effort to try to see other people's points of view. Wherever you interact with others, you can learn, but only if you try to do so.

TWENTY-FOUR HOURS A DAY

Learning how to learn is no great achievement. So said the man quoted at the beginning of this chapter, and many another person would agree with him. Anyone who masters an art completely is likely to underestimate its difficulty. Since this man's mind has been habitually active for many years, he uses it effectively and well. Learning has become a regular and continuous part of his life.

Actually education is a great deal more complicated than he suggested, as we shall see in later chapters. But nothing else matters very much if one does not heed the advice he gave. Everyone does indeed get twenty-four hours a day to spend, and the quality of one's life ultimately depends in part on the systematic and continuing use of some of those hours to learn under the best conditions possible.

Chapter 5

Learning Is Doing

Suppose you are a teacher. You usually devote your class time to lectures, discussion, questions and answers, and student reports. But during one period of the course, you decide to use a film because it very aptly presents an idea you want to convey. Your students reap an immediate advantage because they find it refreshing to do something different and because most people like to see movies. Interest is therefore aroused at once as the students focus their minds on the new experience.

You can increase their learning by doing two things in addition to showing the film. First, you can prepare the students for what they are to see, laying a background for the ideas to be presented and suggesting the points to be looked for or the questions which the film will answer. Second, you can lead a discussion of the film afterward, letting everyone express his views about the major ideas it has presented. These two activities encourage the students to be more active than they would have been otherwise. Their minds interact with the film before, during, and after its showing.

In these ways, you (as a teacher) will be using the fundamental principle that learning must be active to be effective. "Learning is doing" say modern psychologists, and wrapped up in their brief sentence is a con-

61

cept basic to all aspects of education, no matter what is to be learned or how. You (as a learner) can use that principle in many different situations. This chapter is devoted to telling you how to do so.

SQ3R

The most sustained, imaginative, and widely known program of teaching university students how to study has been carried on at Ohio State University. After many years' work, Prof. Francis P. Robinson and his colleagues have developed a basic study procedure which has proved to be highly effective. It has five steps (survey, question, read, recite, review), and from their initials comes the name of the method: SQ3R. It is fully described by Professor Robinson in his scholarly book, *Effective Study* [1], which anybody who is seriously interested in improving study techniques is urged to buy and read.

Since the method is most specifically useful for reading nonfiction, particularly textbooks, let us first apply it in that way. Suppose you are sitting down to study a chapter. You already have a clear picture of the overall nature of the whole book and its contents so that you can fit this particular chapter into its broader context. Now what should you do?

1. *Survey* the whole chapter, trying only to get its central structure of ideas in mind. Look carefully at the headings, summary paragraphs, topic sentences, and italicized words. Then turn to the first section of the chapter. Survey it in turn, looking through the paragraphs to get the gist of each, but not trying to absorb details. (The word "survey" is essentially the same as "skim," which is used elsewhere in this book.)

2. Look up from the book and in your mind phrase

a central *question* or questions which seem to be answered by that section. Often you can turn the headings into questions. (If you were reading this section by this method, you might have asked, "What is the meaning of SQ3R?")

3. *Read* the section thoughtfully. Many people make the mistake of taking this step first, trying to get the full meaning without first preparing the way for themselves. To do so is like the teacher's showing an educational film without laying any background for it.

4. Looking away from the book, *recite* the material to yourself, putting its essence into your own words. If possible, make brief written notes. If you are not satisfied with your mastery of the ideas, look back over the section. The purpose of this recitation, whether put down on paper or only thought through in your mind, is to be sure you understand the basic ideas. Do not make a neat summary of them just for the sake of having good notes or of preserving the words of the author in another form. Recitation is a means to an end: to help you remember what the author said.

5. Proceed through the chapter in this fashion, section by section. When you have finished the whole chapter, *review* it. Go back over your notes to get the basic relationship of one section to another. Then, not looking at your notes, see how well you can remember the basic points in each section.

SQ3R sounds complicated at first. It must be carefully learned if it is to become a smooth, natural process. Once mastered, however, it becomes so automatic you do not need to think about it any more. When one reaches this stage, as the studies at Ohio State show, both the speed and the accuracy of reading increase markedly. An additional benefit for those in formal classes results from the fact that self-questioning helps students prepare for the questions which the professor asks on examinations.

But SQ3R is not just a method for reading textbooks. In essence, it underlies most effective approaches to study. The teacher showing the film helped his students to master its content: he gave them an overview, phrased the questions, showed the film, and then, by discussion, helped in the recitation and review phases.

A discussion group analyzing modern poetry might skim a poem, ask what its essential ideas are, read its text carefully, talk about its structure and meaning, and, at the end, relate it to other poems.

A woman trying to understand music by listening to a series of phonograph records might approach each one in this fashion: She would listen to a composition, paying attention only to its general form and content; ask herself what the composer was trying to do and how he used the disciplines of the form he chose; listen much more carefully; go back over the work to see if she has grasped its essentials; and ponder its relationship to other works studied in the series.

Illustrations could be multiplied but the ones mentioned show how broadly useful SQ3R can be in helping to gain mastery of new material. While the technique cannot always be followed, a person who has it firmly in mind and is inventive in thinking about it will discover its many applications.

TAKING NOTES

The two basic reasons for taking notes have already been suggested: to help you interact with the material at the time you study it, and to help you call its essence back to mind later on. For both purposes, some system for keeping a record of major points is essential. As one woman remarked:

My biggest problem has always been and will always be the inability to retain and in many instances understand the material I have read. I found this out when I first started back to school. The only way I have been able to overcome this problem was to become as proficient as I could in taking down notes.

A major need in taking notes is to have a system for doing so. Bits and fragments of paper with comments recorded as the mood strikes will usually create more confusion than assistance. The best system for most people is to have a sturdily bound loose-leaf notebook filled with an ample supply of paper. Use this paper for all your notes, and keep them filed in an organized fashion.

The central aim in taking notes is to get down the essential ideas in their proper order, stated so that they are clear and intelligible to you both at the time you record them and also later on when you want to use them. You need to compress a textbook, lecture, discussion, reading assignment, or field trip into its essentials, not to keep the fullest possible record of it. Remember that the notes represented *you* interacting with the material. Sometimes a lecturer or a book uses an extremely significant statement which you want to record as it was said or written, but usually everything should be put in your own words.

In most cases, though not in all, the outline form is best for taking notes. Obviously it is a poor method if you are summarizing the plot of a Shakespeare play, recording mathematical formulas, or listing significant dates. But most of the time, writers and lecturers present their material with some emphasis on what is major and what is minor, and they develop each of their points in a logical fashion. You can best record their ideas if you use the same basic system that they have used.

For some reason, outlining is a difficult task for many adults, including some who were able to do so easily in school and college. The ability to arrange ideas in terms of relative importance and comprehensiveness is dulled by the passing years, particularly in people who have not kept their minds active. This inability to outline (either mentally or on paper) is often the basic cause of difficulty when adults try to learn. They cannot separate the essential from the trivial or the major point from the examples used to illustrate it. This problem sometimes has far-reaching consequences. For example, one woman kept failing Spanish examinations because the instructor asked the students to read passages in Spanish and summarize them in English. Finally, the instructor realized that the woman did not know how to make a good summary. When she was given training in outlining, she had no more difficulty.

If you suspect that you are not as effective in outlining as you should be, there are several things you can do. You can take a basic English refresher or study skills course. You can seek specialized tutoring from an English teacher. You can secure a high school or college textbook with a section on outlining and work through its exercises by yourself. You can try outlining nonfiction pieces in books and magazines and ask a friend to check them over for you, if you have confidence in his ability to do so. You can compare your own notes from a class lecture or a text with those of another person who seems more capable than you are. Often, two or more people can check each other's work and thereby render mutual aid.

In these and other ways, the ability to outline can eventually become so automatic that one no longer needs to think about it. Continuing practice is needed until this point is reached. W. A. Barton [2] has shown in an experiment that students taught to outline showed immediate improvement. When they continued to practice this skill for a month, they showed a marked superiority over untrained students.

In taking notes at a class or a lecture, however, one cannot always follow the outline form. The discussion may wander though it touches on all the important points, and lecturers are not always noted for the clarity of their presentation. It is usually wise to follow the practice of one man who said, "After each class period, I go home and immediately condense my notes for that period of time into outline form." This general procedure is excellent, for it provides an immediate review of the material and produces better notes for later use.

Note-taking from a printed source is both easier and more dangerous than note-taking in class. The ease comes from the fact that the book is likely to be well organized. Also, you can go back and forth in it as much as you wish. The danger comes from the fact that you may find yourself merely copying out topic sentences or striking points. Ideas flow from the printed page to the handwritten notebook without ever passing through the mind.

Often you may need to combine notes from various sources. There are several ways to do so.

One is to make a master outline from the text, leaving large quantities of blank space. Then ideas from class, from outside reading, or from other learning experiences can be filled in, thereby making a comprehensive system.

Another is to divide the course into units or topics and make a separate section of the notebook for each one. Then the notes from various sources can be grouped.

Still another is to keep the notes from various sources separate, but to provide a cross-reference system. For example, when your class notes deal with some subject, you can add a notation saying where additional material is to be found on that subject in your text notes or your outside reading notes.

An excellent supplementary method is that described by one man:

> The most useful technique I have found is to take a large sheet of drawing paper and outline the notes taken during the semester—I do this at midterm and at semester time. This way I can look at one sheet of paper and follow the progress of the course, grasping the general viewpoint and the meaning of the material studied.

Whatever system you use, be sure that you are its master. There is no point in making a beautifully complete and highly organized set of notes unless the process of making it or using it is beneficial to you. The proper place for new ideas is not on paper but in your mind.

REINFORCING AND ADMONISHING THE AUTHOR

Another major way of taking notes is to do so directly on the printed material which you are reading—assuming that you own it and are free to do with it as you will. When you want to get the essence of a book, whether you are reading it for a class or on a reading program of your own, you will find it useful to underline significant passages and, if you disagree with the author or find him lacking, to tell him so on the margins or on the blank pages.

Never underline on a first reading of the material. You cannot decide what is of major importance in a section or a chapter until you have read it all and thereby absorbed its essential structure. In the SQ3R method, underlining is a form of recitation, not of reading. After you have gone over the material carefully, go back through it, looking for the major sentences or key phrases and underline them. Be careful not to underline too much. If you do, you will not separate the essential from the trivial. Also, underlining can get to be an end in itself. Fingers can keep on drawing lines after the brain has ceased to function.

Then think about what the author has said. If you agree, tell him why. Do not just put an exclamation mark or "how true!" or "good point" in the margin. Summarize what you like best about what he says. Do not always accept his words as being the absolute and ultimate authority on the subject. Books are written not by God-like beings but by poor humans hunched over typewriters or desks, organizing and presenting their material as best they can, even as you do when you must write a paper. When you read a book, be sure first to get the author's meaning. Then ask yourself whether he is right or complete. If he isn't, record his deficiencies in your notes.

If you are studying for serious mastery, underlining is usually not adequate to provide complete retention. This point was made very well by a corporation executive taking a course in management:

> I like reading the material thoroughly first and then going over it again, underlining the important ideas in red pencil. If I have adequate time, I find that putting the gist of the matter on paper in as close to my own words as possible promotes the most complete retention and understanding of the material possible to me.

REVIEWING

Many comments have already been made about reviewing, but the subject is so important that it deserves special attention. In the psychological study of learning, one of the most fully proved principles is that memory is greatly aided by review. We start forgetting what we have learned almost immediately after we learn it. This is why, as was mentioned in Chapter 4, the sooner a subject is reviewed after it is first learned, the better it will be remembered. Periodic review provides for that overlearning which is so essential for retention.

The essence of reviewing comes not in letting your eyes wander once more over the same old notes but in rethinking whatever it is you are trying to learn. The less routine the repetition, the better. See the subject matter in a new perspective. Reconsider it in terms of your constantly enlarging framework of knowledge. Look for new applications of general points. Test your memory by looking away from the material and reviewing what it says; then look back again to see how well you did. Ask yourself questions about the topic; then see how well you can answer them.

Adults can often put their learning into immediate practice and thereby, in a sense, review it by constant repetition. A labor leader can use the principles of collective bargaining he is studying; a farmer can try out the new techniques the county agent has demonstrated; a housewife can experiment (if her family permits) with the recipes in her course in gourmet cooking. Also, as already noted, men and women can use many spare moments to reflect about their knowledge and to find new applications for it.

If you have special review sessions in your study schedule, they should be spaced out and not crowded together. Concentrated reviewing is as inefficient as concentrated learning. A systematic program of the sort suggested in Chapter 4 is best.

In your reviewing you should concentrate on two aspects of what you are trying to remember. First, go over the material you have not yet adequately learned to try yet again to get it fixed in your mind. Second, think about the material you already know but need to overlearn. In focusing on either of these two aspects, be selective. Emphasize the essential. You will be greatly helped to do so if your note system is adequate.

Many people like to use group sessions for reviewing, feeling that in this way each member of the group can supplement the other. Such sessions are valuable, but only if emphasis is kept on learning. The group should not let its discussion degenerate into idle conversation or permit the prejudices of each member, rather than his knowledge, to influence the thoughts of the others. Also the purpose should be to review, not to learn. One man has put this last point very well:

> I will only engage in group sessions if the other persons in the group have prepared themselves by adequate study beforehand, and I will benefit *myself* by them. I don't feel I have sufficient time to tutor other students via these discussions who have not spent any time themselves on the course material.

Actually, one good way to review a subject is to teach it to somebody else—but only if you and he both realize that that is what you are doing and do not pretend that you are reviewing material which you both already know.

REMEMBERING WHAT YOU LEARN

Many adults feel that they are especially handicapped because they cannot remember things as well as they did when they were children. This fact may be true. If so, it is usually because they have simply not tried for a very long time to memorize anything or, if they did, they used the wrong techniques. The child has a certain advantage in seeing everything with fresh eyes and an impressionable mind. But the adult has an advantage of his own: his far greater range of knowledge. The proper use of this knowledge is the key to memorizing in adulthood.

Sometimes we forget simply because memory fades away. We have not overlearned sufficiently to retain the desired learning. A bright carpet exposed every day to the sun streaming through a window will gradually grow dim and its pattern indistinct. In the same way, time erodes the sharpness and distinctness of our memory. In childhood, we may learn all five verses of a hymn and be able to sing it through faultlessly time after time. But if we do not sing that hymn for a quarter century and then try to do so again, we are likely to be able to remember only a few lines and phrases. Our voices come through strongly on them—but we must hum the rest.

Sometimes we forget because we do not fully grasp the significant essence or central principle of the material we want to remember. Then, later on, when we try to recall, we put together the few facts which remain in our memory into some new pattern which is completely wrong. An old story illustrates this fact. Mr. Jones met Mr. Lummock. "Aha," said Mr. Jones to himself, "I'll remember his name all right; it rhymes with stomach!" But a few weeks passed before Mr. Jones saw his new acquaintance again. "Well, hello," he exclaimed. "It's good to see you, Mr.—uh—uh—Mr. Kelly!"

The process of memory often makes use of logical frameworks. Suppose a student of English literature is asked to identify the author and title of the work in which the following quotation appears:

> Not Amurath an Amurath succeeds
> But Harry Harry.

He may be able to spot it at once simply because he remembers where it occurs and how powerful a meaning it has there. But suppose he doesn't remember. Then he must engage in a process of deduction. It is blank verse. The word "Amurath" calls up no memories. The word "succeed" seems to imply the replacing of one king by another. But there are no well-known kings named "Harry." Could this be a nickname? When did one king with this nickname succeed another one with the same nickname? Could it be Henry IV and Henry V of England? What author wrote about this succession? Shakespeare. Where? In *Henry IV*, Part 2. And here the memory of the scene floods back: of the young king assuming his new station in life (he is no longer gay Prince Hal), giving reassurance that he is not an oriental despot prepared to punish all his enemies but a reasonable and decent Englishman who seeks peace.

The steps in this deduction have been spelled out. As the process actually occurs, it is likely not to plod step by step in this fashion but to proceed by a sudden leap forward in which the mind perceives the answer and then works out the logical reasons, testing the initial guess to see if it appears sound, and finally concluding that it does.

A student not as well grounded might go astray at many points. He might focus on the word "Amurath," confuse it with some other name like it ("Tamerlane," perhaps), and come up with an epic in which that name occurs. Or he might misread "succeeds" to be the opposite of "fails" and put down the name of a poem in which there is a great race. As for "Harry"—well, there are many characters with that name scattered all through literature. The student picks the first one he thinks of and puts down the name of the work in which Harry is a leading character. In these latter cases, a logical framework was grasped at—but it was the wrong one.

Broadly speaking, everything in this book is intended

to provide an aid to memory, which is, in some sense, part of all learning. But sometimes memorizing is an essentially separate activity, as when one learns a poem or a piece of music, the vocabulary of a foreign language, or the classification of plants. In any such situation, the following suggestions may be of help.

1. Intend to remember. Give the new fact your full attention at the time you are introduced to it, expecting that you will later have to recall it. When you look at a chart or diagram you never expect to use or see again, you may make no effort to remember it. If you expect it to be important in your business career, however, you will focus your attention closely on it. In the second case, you will remember far more than in the first case.

2. If an idea or fact is new to you, be sure you understand it. Don't get just a general vague impression. Unless a topic is sharply clear to you, there is little hope that you will be able to call it back to mind.

3. Repeat the thing to be learned immediately after you learn it. Notice, for example, the way a person who is said to have a fabulous memory for names proceeds. He makes use of all three of these suggestions. He pays attention; he is sure he gets the name correctly (asking that it be spelled if need be), and then he uses it several times almost at once.

4. If you are memorizing a fact, put it into some logical order appropriate to it. For example, you will probably want to remember historical facts by establishing their sequence in time and geographical facts by their distribution in space.

5. If you are memorizing a complex system of ideas, set up internal categories or key words. One of the errors in memorizing is to try to grasp everything at once indiscriminately. If a man conducting a poll were to ask you, "What did you read yesterday?" you might look at him blankly, and say, "Well, nothing much." If

he asked about your reading of newspapers, magazines, books, letters, and pamphlets, his separate questions would unlock a flood of recollections. You can use this principle in memorizing if you use meaningful groupings. Remember painters or writers by the schools to which they belonged. Remember the works of a composer in terms of the musical forms he used, such as operas, symphonies, piano concertos, and string quartets.

6. If you have an extended work to memorize, such as a poem or a biological classification, try this technique. First, read the whole work aloud several times to get its basic form in your mind. Then, go at it section by section. As you feel you have each section memorized, add it to the earlier sections and repeat to yourself all that you have learned so far. When you have finished, overlearn the work by repeating it again and again. There are other methods of memorizing a long work, such as learning it piece by piece and then putting all of the pieces together, or trying to learn the whole work without breaking it up into sections. One of these methods possibly may be better for you than the combined-whole-and-part method, but if you don't have a preference, try that method first for it is probably the best technique for most people.

7. Space extended memorization over a number of different sessions.

8. Pay special attention to ideas or points of view with which you disagree. Darwin said he had to write down anything in opposition to his theories or he was sure to forget it. Remember the basic rule suggested in Chapter 3—keep in mind the strength of your own point of view.

9. Use an artificial memory system only if there is no meaningful inherent pattern. Millions of people (you may be one of them) when asked how many days there are in August must either say over a children's

jingle or count months out on their knuckles. The letters of the spaces in the treble clef make up the word FACE, and the lines assure you that Every Good Boy Does Fine. Many of the widely advertised memory systems use tricks of this sort.

There is nothing wrong with artificial systems if they are wisely and sparingly used, but tricks can sometimes get in the way of real learning. They have no inherent meaning, so they become excess baggage. Why should you have to say over a rhyme to yourself before you can remember how many days August has? Sometimes, too, these tricks interfere with meaningful learning. A generation ago, a conductor teaching music appreciation on the radio wanted his audience of children to remember the striking theme from the prelude to *Die Meistersinger*, so he set words to it which began "King David with his harp and shield—." Now King David has nothing to do with *Die Meistersinger* and the prelude was not meant to have words. Nevertheless, there are probably many middle-aged Americans today who, when they hear the bold chords sound forth, think vaguely about King David.

Underlying all suggestions of specific techniques lies the fundamental fact that men and women can remember best if they fit their new knowledge meaningfully into what they already know. As William James [3] put it, ". . . of two men with the same outward experiences and the same amount of mere native tenacity, *the one who THINKS over his experiences most*, and weaves them into systematic relations with each other, *will be the one with the best memory*."

LEARNING NEW SKILLS

Most adult learning has to do with facts, ideas, and understanding, but sometimes it is necessary for adults to become proficient in a new skill. Usually they find it hard to do so, particularly when what they want to know requires physical dexterity. (Remember Mr. Bergan trying to learn to play the piano?) As every senior citizen's center shows, however, men and women do acquire new skills, even at a very advanced age.

What happens during the process of learning skills was analyzed by William F. Book [4] in a famous study. The skill concerned was typewriting, which is so commonplace a task that many people do not realize how complicated it is until they think about how many different processes are required to turn out rapidly a piece of correct and attractive copy.

The beginning typist has to think letter by letter. If he wants to write "the," he must painstakingly find the *t* and then the *h* and then the *e*. But the typist who does sixty words a minute (and most words contain more than three letters) has only a second for each one. He cannot think about the separate letters but only about a whole word or, indeed, a group of words. He inserts the carbon paper between the sheets, rolls them into the typewriter, adjusts the margin and the spacing, and is off in a flash, using the special equipment and devices of the typewriter without thinking about them. In seven or eight minutes, he has completed a page of clear, clean copy. In the same time, the beginner will have put in the pages all crooked, failed to adjust the margin, and laboriously pecked out a single line of messy copy, with some letters struck too hard and others too softly, and with many mistakes.

How do you get from the stage of the beginner to the stage of the accomplished professional, as hundreds of thousands of people do each year? Dr. Book, using precise measuring instruments, followed the course of learning of a number of people and came to some interesting conclusions.

First, he points out that "the special habits involved in the mastery of typewriting, though all developing together, are not actually driven abreast. Their manner of growth is something like the movement of a flock of sheep along a country road. The whole flock moves forward, now faster and now slower, while now this and now that particular sheep pushes ahead of the rest." In the early days of learning to type, progress is fairly rapid because the beginner is making advances "along many different lines at once. Rapid strides of improvement are possible and made simultaneously in every department of the work." As time goes on, the number of possibilities of improvement begin to decline "until, as still more skill is acquired, a state is reached where most adaptations or short cuts in method have been made; fewer special habits remain to be developed; fewer adaptations are possible. Those possible have become harder and harder to make, because they must be made in the realm of higher habits where the learner has had less experience. Every man has had experience with the first stages of learning, but little with the later stages because most people touch lightly many things and are masters of nothing."

Pause now and reflect on the last skill you learned? Was it the preparation of complete meals for your family? Was it driving a car? Was it learning to play a game, such as golf, tennis, bridge, or bowling? Was it acquiring a new foreign language? In any such case, you will see how basic to your own experience is the account which Dr. Book gave to learning just such a complicated skill. At the beginning, there were an incredible number of matters to be thought of all at once, but gradually you got most of them under some kind of control. Then you started refining them one by one. Finally, at some stage of the game, you were satisfied. You had reached the amount of mastery you felt you wanted. That was enough. Progress stopped.

By what stages does the improvement of skills occur? Dr. Book was as aware as the rest of us that occasionally people practice and practice but seem to make no progress. At other times they move forward rapidly. Why is this true?

The answer seems to be that progress first comes naturally, without our willing it to do so, but that it does not become established at a high level without conscious and sustained effort. "All adaptations and short cuts in method," said Dr. Book, "were . . . fallen into by the learners quite unintentionally on the good days while practicing under strain. The learners suddenly noticed that they were doing certain parts of the work in a new and better way, then purposely adopted it in the future." The typist, for example, after laboriously pecking out letter after letter suddenly found that he was occasionally focusing on syllables or whole words. This practice increased his speed, so he deliberately forced himself to use the new technique. Before long, he was doing so naturally.

But customary ways of doing things are hard to change. "At every lapse in attention or relaxation of effort, the older habits stepped forward, as it were, and assumed control, thereby tending to perpetuate themselves. Only when a high degree of efficient effort was being persistently applied, only when the learners were urging themselves forward so hard that these outgrown habits had no chance to be used was attention forced to lay hold of the higher and more economical methods of work. . . ."

And, of course, when attention and effort are relaxed, "the learner settles down to more primitive methods of work, writing on a low plane when closer attention and increased effort would mean new adaptations, rapid improvement, and the development of more advanced methods of work." And so, if progress is to continue, the learner's "attention must be kept sharply focused on the details of the work and continually pushed out on the frontier where new adaptations in method can be laid hold of."

From Book's research, and from other studies as well, specific suggestions may be made.

1. Practice as hard as you can, faithfully, persistently, and with a will to improve. Begin practicing as soon as you can, even though your knowledge or ability is still imperfect. Anything worth doing is worth doing badly—at first!

2. As you practice, reflect about what you are doing. When you see that you have naturally acquired a way of doing something which seems to bring better results, stress that new habit.

3. Put the skill you are trying to learn into words, thereby fixing it more sharply in your mind. If you are learning to water-ski, for example, your instructor will not only show you how to rise erect as the boat takes off but will also tell you what to do. Repeat the instruction as you imitate the action.

4. Realize that every complicated skill is really a "flock" of habits and that good performance is the ability to perform all of them at once. Therefore, think about the deficiencies in your practice and concentrate on them. Perhaps, for example, the reason your Swedish is difficult to understand is that you have not fully mastered the vowel sounds. Study how to say them and do so consciously until they have become so natural to your speech that you no longer need to think about them.

5. If you can do so, keep a chart or graph showing your progress. In studying typing, for example, your scores on speed tests can provide the basis for a continuing record. You can see how well you are doing— and also what score you must beat if you are to continue to increase your skill.

6. If your chart seems to level off though you are doing your best to improve, don't be discouraged. Such plateaus occur in most learning patterns. Probably you are going through some shift in your basic

habits which, when you have fully absorbed it, will lead to a rising line again.

7. Eliminate the extra habits which hold back your progress. A beginning tennis player runs about on the court, flails his racket wildly, and visibly tenses up as he sees the ball coming over the net. The accomplished player's movements are so smooth and flowing that he makes everything look easy. If you have trouble progressing, analyze your performance (or, better still, ask an expert to do so) and find out in what ways you are defeating yourself.

8. As far as possible, practice in natural settings and with realistic materials. A man learning to serve in tennis will find that in real games he acquires an ability to adjust to the condition of the court, the shifting wind and light, and his opponents' probable returns. Serving 500 times in such varying conditions provides him with a much more flexible service than do 500 practice serves delivered up monotonously one after the other without continuing to play.

9. Realize that when you no longer use the general plan of attack enumerated above, your competence will level off. It may even decline as you slip back into bad habits.

CONCLUSION

This chapter has dealt chiefly with the learning of facts, ideas, and skills which make possible all the deeper and broader kinds of learning so significant to a good life. Consider, for example, this poem by Francis William Bourdillon [5]:

> The night has a thousand eyes,
>   And the day but one;
> Yet the light of the bright world dies
>   With the dying sun.

The mind has a thousand eyes,
  And the heart but one;
Yet the light of a whole life dies
  When love is done.

This little poem is so beautiful and so piercingly true that it has an immediate impact on the reader, despite its simplicity. It uses twenty-seven different words, of which only two are longer than one syllable. And yet appreciation of it depends on seemingly simple but actually complex facts, skills, and ideas, such as the ability to read, the understanding of the meaning of each of the words, the realization that "eyes" refers in one place to stars and in another to thoughts, and the ability to perceive the power and exactness of the metaphor used. Until these conditions are met, it is impossible to enjoy the poem.

In this introductory book, which deals only with the essentials, there is not enough room to explore all the various ways by which adults can be helped to think creatively, to acquire new attitudes and points of view, or to develop an appreciation of the good things of the world. These goals are so subtle that each requires special guidance. The only thing that may be said about them here is that they should be actively sought by every adult who hopes to develop his potentialities more fully. In achieving them, as in trying to reach simpler goals, learning is doing.

Chapter 6

Getting More from Your Reading

"Some subjects are more important than others," observed John W. Gardner [1]. "Reading is the most important of all." This comment has high authority, for it appeared in the *Report of the President's Commission on National Goals,* and its author is the head of the Carnegie Corporation. Everyone who understands the processes of education would agree. Reading is the skill which supports all other methods of learning, enlarges the horizons of the mind, permits us to move freely across space and time to establish contact with those with whom we have a community of interest, and corrects the distorted or narrow views which we often get from first-hand observation and from other methods of learning.

To some degree, you already accept the values of reading or you would not be using this book. You may not have a broad enough idea, however, about how to gain more of those values for yourself. Let us put the matter to the test. When you read the title of this chapter, did you think that the way by which you could get more out of reading would be by increasing your speed?

If you answered that question "yes," there is a good chance you were right. Most people can indeed increase their reading speed. But if "reading improvement" and "increasing the speed of reading" coalesce in your mind, you are falling subject to a widespread error which has been drummed into the minds of many modern adults by the great publicity given to "new systems" that promise fantastically rapid speeds and by the success stories of individuals who dramatically increased their reading rates. Such accounts leave most of us feeling vaguely uncomfortable. We think we are poking along with horse-and-buggy habits while others, in their sleek automobiles, roar past. We must not be deluded! Speed is important but only if it gets us to the proper destination.

One of the wisest of men, Sir Francis Bacon [2], remarked more than three centuries ago, "Reading maketh a full man; conference a ready man; and writing an exact man." The next two chapters will deal with writing and with conference. This chapter will be about reading. The first aim is to discuss the nature of the skill itself and how to improve your competence in it. The second aim is to suggest how you can best use reading to enlarge your knowledge, your understanding, and your appreciation—to become, to use Bacon's word, a "full" man or woman.

READING STYLES

The first important fact to realize about reading is that the way we use the skill should be determined by what we hope to get from it. We read for countless reasons: to follow traffic signals, to learn calculus, to keep up with the comics, to escape into a dream life, to know what is going on in the world, to carry on a business transaction, to understand the word of God, to learn how to make a backyard barbecue, to find a telephone number, to acquire a deeper appreciation of poetry. . . . Since purposes and motives are infinitely varied, so are the ways we read. Yet there are several basic reading styles, each used to achieve a multitude of different goals.

One of these is *reading for mastery of content*. Some people assume that this style is the only one, and it is, indeed, the major way of reading for those who hope to learn. The basic purpose is to absorb the facts and ideas expressed by the author, who makes available the results of his work and his scholarship. This reading style is, in most cases, best carried out by the SQ3R technique described at the beginning of Chapter 5. (Note the fact that comprehension is not directly linked to speed, even within a given style. In using SQ3R, one first reads very rapidly, then pauses, then reads more slowly, and after two more steps, reads rapidly again.)

A second style is *reading to gain the central idea*. In a sense, this style is but the first part of the technique used when reading for mastery of content. There we intend to return for a closer reading. Sometimes, however, we can get all we want from a book by a quick survey of its title, preface, table of contents, and subject headings, and by running our eyes rapidly down the pages of print. We get the gist of it—and that is enough. A student confronted with twenty books on a reading list to be covered in limited time can skim them all and then go back to read more carefully only those which will be most rewarding.

A third style is *reading to discover a fact or facts*. Here is another kind of skimming, in which the purpose is not to get a central idea but to dig out a particular fact. Suppose, in reading about SQ3R just now, you happened to think that you do not remember what word the final *R* stands for. Perhaps you went back to the beginning of Chapter 5 (which you were cued to do because it was mentioned at that point) and hastily looked down the pages until finally the word "review" almost leaped into your notice. This kind of reading is common in everyday life as we look up telephone numbers, weather forecasts, or times of television shows. It is also a frequently used style in studying, for often one needs to go back from time to time to pick up again a forgotten point.

A fourth style is *reading to know how to follow directions*. Sometimes this style requires very slow reading, as you will realize if you think about how complex a recipe or a set of plans for building a piece of furniture can be. You must work your way slowly through a compressed and often dense set of instructions. Many a father has gone completely to pieces late on Christmas eve when informed that he should "insert rod at point A and attach to center part of ratchet which should first be placed in position indicated in diagram 3A (if you are building Model 243) or diagram 3B (if you are building Model 244)."

The second, third, and fourth styles are, in a sense, merely special applications of the first. The fifth is essentially different. It is *reading for enjoyment*. Here the purpose is to appreciate the material read, whatever it may be. Ideally we become completely absorbed in what we are reading. If it is fiction, the characters come alive and what happens to them really matters. If it is poetry, we are caught up by the language. The rate of reading is determined largely by the nature of the material and by our capacity to react to it. We may move rapidly over some sections which seem less interesting than others. We may consciously slow down in the last pages just because we do not want the delightful association to end.

There are other kinds of reading styles which are either different from these five or are variants of them. (For example, reading for escape, in which we try to drive away cares by turning to detective stories or tales of the wild west, is very like reading for enjoyment and yet, in some ways, different from it.) The important thing is not to list all possible styles but to realize that each determines the amount we read, the speed with which we read it, and what we get from the process.

HOW THE MATERIAL INFLUENCES YOUR READING

The second factor governing the reading process is the material read—its basic nature, its inherent difficulty, and its interest to the reader. There are as many different kinds of things to be read as there are reasons for reading them. The way materials influence reading, however, can be suggested by mentioning six different types.

Most studying occurs through the use of *organized nonfiction*, of which a textbook is a good example. Here the author has brought his material into a coherent outline, moving logically from one topic to the next, with carefully constructed paragraphs, each of which has sentences put together in the proper order. This kind of material is usually the easiest to master, for the author has tried to help you put every idea into proper perspective.

Much of what we read, however, is *discursive nonfiction,* such as a letter from a friend. In informal writing of this sort, the author does not bother to organize his thoughts. He rambles along from one topic to another, as each strikes his fancy. Your reading must go along with him in the same spirit. Some of the world's great literature is written in this fashion. An essay by Montaigne, for example, is a series of sharp and penetrating sentences, each of which must be read on its own terms for the satisfaction it brings. Here was a wise and witty man, setting down his thoughts as they came to him, only loosely grouping them together into broad topics. If you try to skim one of his essays, you will miss the whole point of what he was trying to do.

Fiction, in either prose or verse, must also be approached on its own terms. Its author may intend to tell a story, to portray a character or a setting, to illustrate a point of ethics, or to fulfill some other purpose. Often fiction can be read at several different levels. *Huckleberry Finn,* for example, is a good and gripping story. It also brings alive almost every character it deals with. It describes the way of life of an important part of the country as it existed in a bygone era. It uses language in a wholly original way. In the history of literature, it holds an important place as perhaps the first completely American book, untouched by European influence. Some critics would say it is the greatest novel yet written in this country. Such a book is approached and read for enjoyment and understanding in several different ways, all of which are different from the methods used for either organized or discursive nonfiction.

Poetry comes in many forms. Sometimes it is very like prose fiction; such is the case with "Hiawatha" or "Evangeline." But in poetry, the language itself is always significant. The poet tries by eloquence, rhythm, structure, and other means not merely to convey his ideas but to do so in a powerful and compelling fashion. (The idea of the poem appearing on pages 81 to 82 can be expressed as follows: Intellectual brilliance is worth nothing without love. You will agree that Bourdillon said it better!) When you read a poem, therefore, you must always pay attention to its language and its form as well as to what it says.

Mathematics is a special language which must be read carefully and exactly. Each number used is a precise quantity, and each symbol has a single meaning. You must first therefore learn the language. Even after you do so, you must read it with full attention to detail.

Finally, *tables, graphs, charts, maps, and other similar forms of representation* must also be read in a special way. On a table, for example, one must understand the heading, the columns, the units of measurement, and the intervals of time or quantity for which the data are presented. These matters can be bothersome to the uninitiated, but tables can compress data in a marvelously compact and revealing way. Most people find it well worth taking time to learn the special skills required to read them as well as the other forms of representation of data.

The kind of material, then, is important in determining the speed and nature of reading. Each calls for a somewhat different pattern of skills. This difference is made even greater by the fact that in each kind there are many levels of inherent difficulty.

Some books are easy to read! You pick them up with joy. They grip you with their excitement. You get their meaning at once. They help you make your own life more happy and glamorous. Other volumes develop complex and integrated patterns of interrelated thought in a fundamental and basic exposition of verities which are undeniably relevant to the continuing *summum bonum* of humanity; they express profundities of human experience which are unequivocally universal although in each particular elucidation they must be seen as being deeply and perhaps inextricably related to socio-politico-economic realities within a particular ethnocentrism; and they are hard to read.

You get the point, of course. Some writers say things simply, by the use of brief sentences, short and colorful words, and a direct approach to the reader. These devices, when poorly used, can produce an irritating style (like that used at the start of the last paragraph) which tells the reader that the author is talking down to him. Other writers use a gray, complicated style, even worse than that employed at the end of the last paragraph.

Your ability to get meaning from what you read and to do so rapidly depends partly therefore on the inherent difficulty of the material. This is true whether it is in standard English, in any of the vocabularies used in various fields of knowledge (such as economics or physics), or in the special language of mathematics. In all of these cases, there are various levels of difficulty, and improvement of the ability to read may depend on ability to reach the higher levels. As Patrick Meredith [3] once observed, "Language is a kind of smokey, crinkly glass through which the author is trying to signal you. Your task is to see through the language to the meanings."

Difficulty and complexity of language is never good for its own sake, but both are sometimes necessary to express an idea. To refer yet again to Bourdillon's poem, it is apparent that one of its virtues is its simplicity. Contrast it with a poem by Gerard Manley Hopkins [4] called "Pied Beauty":

> Glory be to God for dappled things—
>> For skies of couple-colour as a brinded cow;
> For rose-moles all in stipple upon trout that swim;
> Fresh-firecoal chestnut-falls; finches' wings;
>> Landscape plotted and pieced—fold, fallow, and
>>> plough;
>> And áll trádes, their gear and tackle and trim.
>
> All things counter, original, spare, strange;
>> Whatever is fickle, freckled (who knows how?)
>> With swift, slow; sweet, sour; adazzle, dim;
> He fathers-forth whose beauty is past change:
>> Praise him.

The basic idea of this poem is no more strange or complex than that of the earlier, simpler one. But Hopkins's idea can best be expressed by the use of an intricate structure of language with strange words put together in an unusual way. Bourdillon used one powerful metaphor. Hopkins uses at least thirteen, perhaps more.

The reading of Hopkins's poem must be an entirely different process from the reading of Bourdillon's. In the latter case, your eyes sweep quickly over the eight lines and get its meaning at once. You may need to go back to pick up one or two extra qualities you missed the first time, but the meaning of the poem is almost instantly clear. With "Pied Beauty," the idea is obvious in the first line, though the word "dappled" is unusual enough to signal you that the poem will have originality of expression. If you are to enjoy the full development of the poem, however, you must go over it again and again. The language expresses an unusual thought in a distinctive way, and the poem introduces you to the complex genius of its author. Only gradually can the rich diversity of both be revealed to you.

You may say that difficult reading is too much trouble, that you will stay with the simple things. If so, you are locking yourself away from some of the richest treasures of mankind, for some ideas are so complex and subtle that they cannot be expressed except in difficult language.

Still another way by which the material itself influences your reading of it is: How interesting is it to you? Interest is always related to the person and the occasion. One man may turn to a page of mathematical formulas with the keenest relish while another goes to almost any length to avoid them. On some occasions, one is more interested in a subject than on others. For example, a recipe usually has the absorbed attention of the housewife who is following it, while at other times she is indifferent to it.

Some material, however, is written in such a way as to be generally interesting. It does not necessarily use the special devices of simple writing, such as short sentences, one-syllable words, colorful adjectives, and anecdotes. Yet somehow it captures the attention. The following passage has seemed to many people to have this quality:

> Five hundred years before Christ in a little town on the far western border of the settled and civilized world, a strange new power was at work. Something had awakened in the minds and spirits of the men there which was so to influence the world that the slow passage of long time, of century upon century, and the shattering changes they brought, would be powerless to wear away that deep impress. Athens had entered upon her brief and magnificent flowering of genius which so molded the world of mind and of spirit that our mind and spirit today are different. We think and feel differently because of what a little Greek town did during a century or two, twenty-four hundred years ago. What was then produced of art and of thought has never been surpassed and very rarely equalled, and the stamp of it is upon all the art and all the thought of the Western world. And yet this full stature of greatness came to pass at a time when the mighty civilizations of the ancient world had perished and the shadow of "effortless barbarism" was dark upon the earth. In that black and fierce world a little centre of white-hot spiritual energy was at work. A new civilization had arisen in Athens, unlike all that had gone before.

This first paragraph from Edith Hamilton's *The Greek Way* [5] uses the talent of a gifted author to arouse the interest of the reader. How did she achieve this effect? If we knew the answer to that question, we would all be able to write books which have the hundreds of thousands of devoted readers that hers have had.

READING COMPREHENSION

The foregoing discussion suggests how varied is the skill to which we give the simple name "reading." Fundamentally, it is the process by which symbols on a page are given meaning by the mind. Sometimes that meaning can be exactly the one intended by the person who wrote the symbols. Such is the case with mathematics and charts. Sometimes the meaning is not precise and clear, but is designed to call forth a rich and diverse response, flowing from the reader's deepest thoughts and memories. Such is the case with poetry and imaginative fiction. Most writing—and, therefore, most reading—lies somewhere between these two extremes.

Your comprehension of what you read depends first of all upon your familiarity with the symbols which the author uses. If you do not know Russian, you would not expect to be able to read a book written in that language. Many people fail to realize, however, that even within English there are many special vocabularies. In most newspapers, the business news is next to the news of sports, yet each uses words never found in the other. Another good example is in the use of maps. To many people, maps are just a way of finding out how to get to one place from another. But to those who really read them, they have far more eloquent meanings.

Recognizing, then, that there are many different special languages, let us concentrate attention on basic or standard English. There are several ways by which, in the ordinary course of study, you can improve your comprehension of what you read.

BUILDING YOUR VOCABULARY

The first way to improve your comprehension is to increase the number of words you know and to learn them so well that you do not even need to think about what they mean. There is no point, of course, in knowing words just for the sake of knowing them, unless your aim is to delight in the range of your knowledge and perhaps to demonstrate it to others. But it is always a wise idea to be curious about words which are not completely familiar to you because you never know when you may encounter them again.

Somewhere on the first two pages of this chapter, there is a word which many people who read this book might not know. *Don't look back at it until you are asked to do so!*

Did you notice this strange word when you read it, and did you wonder what it meant? If so, what did you do? The proper procedure would have been to underline it and move on in your reading in order not to interrupt the flow of your thought. Then you should have gone back later, looked it up in the dictionary, and decided whether you wanted to add it to your vocabulary. If you did want to add it, you should have written it down several times and reviewed its meaning. Then you should have used it two or three times as soon as you could do so naturally. It would have then been yours.

Did you fail to notice an unusual word? Maybe you were skimming at that point and got the meaning of the sentence and the paragraph just by the context; knowledge of the individual word was not necessary. If you were doing a closer reading and didn't know the word, you would have noticed it, but you might still have ignored it since the meaning of the passage was clear anyway. Some day, however, you may come across the word in a context that does not make its meaning so clear. What will you do then? The best thing is not to let words go by but to master them.

You may already have disregarded instructions and gone back to look for the word. If not, please do so now. . . . Did you find it? If so, did you rapidly skim down the pages until it virtually leaped out at you? That was the right way, for you were using a particular kind of reading style. If you tediously reread all the words, you used the wrong style.

Couldn't you find the word at all? That means you already knew it. Congratulations! But there are other pages and other words. For example, as you have reached this point in this chapter, have you understood all the following words: calculus, gist, inherent, coherent, perspective, discursive, uninitiated, metaphor, symbol, and context? Did any of them cause you even a moment's hesitation? If not, once again: Congratulations! But there are other pages and other words.

Everybody occasionally misreads certain words. If a sentence says, "The lithe batter strode to the plate," a few people will almost certainly read "little" instead of "lithe." If the account goes on to say, "Drawing himself up to his full 6 feet 4 inches, he confronted the pitcher," they will realize that something is wrong. Looking back over the passage, they will see their error.

A part of gaining comprehension, then, is the ability to recognize words easily, quickly, and precisely. In essence, we do not even see them as words at all. We "see" their meaning as they are combined with other words. But if we see a meaning which isn't there, we are led astray. Many a bet has been lost because somebody who was *sure* he had read something looked back and found he had read it incorrectly.

If you find yourself having difficulty with word recognition, you are probably not interacting fully enough with the material you are reading. Give it more of your conscious attention. Think about what it means. Every time something seems a bit odd, go back to see if you have misread a word. If the same words keep on giving you trouble, make a list of them or in some other way bring them more consciously to your attention. Do the same thing with words whose meaning you do not know.

UNDERSTANDING THE INNER STRUCTURE

Words are constructed into sentences. To the student of language, a sentence is not just a series of words with a subject and a predicate but the best and clearest exposition of an idea. Recalling when he was a student at Harrow, Winston Churchill [6] said, "I got into my bones the essential structure of the ordinary British sentence—which is a noble thing." To see a series of beautifully constructed sentences, look back to the quotation from Edith Hamilton. They are far from simple but the meaning of each is clear and precise.

The clarity and forcefulness of the sentence is important to the reader. He understands that it conveys a single idea, even though that idea may be complex. He gets the sweep and the drift of the sentence, distinguishing at once, for example, among sentences which say something, sentences which ask something, and sentences which exclaim something.

Organized nonfiction is usually put together in terms of units of thought, each conveyed by a paragraph. The good reader of this kind of material may be initially aware of its concepts paragraph by paragraph rather than sentence by sentence. He will get the central idea and only then see how it has been developed. Sometimes the major idea is stated in what is called a "topic sentence," which is then supplemented by the other sentences, each of which has meaning in terms of the larger whole of the paragraph. Sometimes there is no one topic sentence but you can, if you wish, construct one. In fact, that is what you often do when you take notes.

Paragraphs are but parts of larger units. Sections make up chapters and chapters make up the book. Sometimes the author uses even more levels than these. He may group his chapters, for example, into the major divisions of his work. Ideally, there are many levels of meaning running from the central ideas of the book to the central idea of each sentence, with everything taken together making up a perfectly harmonious whole.

"Ideally" this may be true, but no book quite reaches the ideal. Not even a magazine article or any other short piece can ever live up to all the requirements of perfect construction. The personality of the author controls his work, and what he wants to say usually causes him now and then to abandon a strictly logical form. Still, there is great value in knowing about the ideal. Meaning comes essentially from the way ideas are put together. The author of organized nonfiction, if he is competent, knows what is expected of him and tries to live up to that expectation. He enters into an agreement with his readers that he will structure his thoughts and convey them by the way he writes his divisions, chapters, sections, paragraphs, and sentences. But he is not a machine. He is a man who is trying to say something and who cannot always do so in a completely coherent fashion.

In the other forms of material mentioned earlier, meaning also comes from the way ideas are put together. A short story has an inner logic, which is usually more subtle than that of a nonfiction article. Poetry is even more complex. A poem may be presented in an established form—a sonnet, a triolet, a ballade— and it is useful to know what that form usually means. In a sonnet, for example, tradition requires that the first eight lines shall be different in some striking way from the last six, perhaps moving from the general to the specific or from passiveness to activeness.

In appreciating any kind of reading material, an awareness of form is important. We gain meaning from each particular example because we know the rules by which it has been constructed, and we gain even more delight when the rules are occasionally violated. In "Pied Beauty," Hopkins gains great power by the simplicity of his last line. Two emotion-charged syllables are given the same weight that in the other lines is carried by from nine to twelve syllables.

DETECTING THE WRITER'S POINT OF VIEW

As noted earlier, authors always have points of view and express them whether they want to or not. Sometimes they want to very much indeed! Much of what we read is intended to get us to do something—vote for a man or a party, buy a brand of baked beans, smoke a particular kind of cigarette, or have our cars greased every thousand miles. This urging is sometimes so extreme that it does not fool even young children. On the television commercial, a movie star may drink a particular kind of ginger ale with great relish, but his six-year-old audience meanwhile makes loud throwing-up noises.

Now the star may or may not drink ginger ale and, if so, he may or may not drink that particular brand. A few people will perhaps be fooled and buy the ginger ale because a specific movie star is shown drinking it.

But the advertiser is trying to get across a more general message: My ginger ale is the one which well-known people drink. The advertiser knows that if time after time enough people see his product being consumed by the famous, the basic idea may gradually sink in. As a result, you will someday (he hopes) pick up a bottle of his brand rather than the one you have been drinking and not even know why you do so.

Persuasion can occur without the author's departing in any respect from the truth, just by the way he writes. Look at these two passages:

> The room was shabby and threadbare, with books and magazines piled everywhere, showing the owner's lack of any regard for order or neatness.

> The shabbiness of the room and its threadbare furniture bore mute witness that its owner was not concerned with material things; the abundance of books and magazines scattered everywhere spoke eloquently of his love for higher things, for the life of the mind.

Both authors provide their readers with the same facts, but create very different effects. Their viewpoints may have been unconscious in both cases; it is possible neither author was deliberately trying to lead his reader's thoughts in one direction or the other. To one, neatness was important. To the other, the evidence of the use of books and magazines was significant. The language simply reflected what each thought.

Most material that adults read is slanted in some direction, either intentionally or not. You cannot comprehend what you read, therefore, unless you make allowance for the author's bias. Watch his language for the colored words which subtly convey his values. See how he has arranged the facts to put his own interpretation on them. Try occasionally to think how the same basic data would look to somebody else.

The best way to correct for narrowness and a slanted point of view is to read several accounts of the same facts. One author may stress the importance of slavery as a cause of the Civil War. Another will emphasize the differences between an agricultural South and an industrializing North. If you want a balanced view, therefore, you must read both, and probably a number of others as well. If you have been reading a liberal newspaper, you have probably absorbed its views. It might be a good idea for a while then also to read a conservative newspaper to see how differently it covers the news.

To sum up, comprehension of reading is aided by many capacities, of which the most important are these: an understanding of the words or other symbols used; an ability to recognize them exactly without thinking about them; an understanding of the basic structure of the particular material read; and a sensitiveness to the arts of persuasion. The good reader must possess all these capacities.

IMPROVING YOUR READING COMPETENCE

Most sciences are built on basic new findings. The discovery of microbes made possible the attack against disease. The demonstration that the earth revolves around the sun opened up the study of the solar system. Just such a fundamental disclosure made possible modern techniques for the improvement of reading. People had assumed that this skill was essentially a process by which the eyes moved steadily across a line of print, looking at letter after letter which the mind automatically grouped into words. When one line was finished, the eye swept back to the start of the next one. But a closer look at the facts revealed that this assumption was wrong.

The normal eye does not sweep across the line of print continuously but moves in a series of jerks. In between jerks, the eye is focused on a part of the line. (Each such period is called a fixation.) When the mind has absorbed that part, the eye jerks on. Ordinarily the motion is so swift that one has no sense of the jerks at all, any more than one has of the individual pictures in a movie. But Paul D. Leedy [7], in his book *Reading Improvement for Adults,* describes how you can actually see these movements:

> With an ordinary pin, puncture the page at the center. Have the reader face toward a source of light which will illuminate his face, especially his eyes. Stand facing the reader. Hold the page with the pinhole in it at eye level. Sight through the pinhole. Ask the person to read the printed matter on the other side of the page. Watch carefully through the pinhole. You will see the reader's eyes move across the line with little jerks and stops. At the end of each line, you will see his eyes swing back to the beginning of the next line.

The scientific basis of good reading skill is to make these eye movements more efficient in several ways:

1. The number of fixations per line is reduced. The eye is encouraged to look at print, not letter by letter or even word by word, but in terms of groups of words. A good reader might have only about three fixations per line. A poor reader might have twenty or more.

2. The time spent on each fixation is reduced, thereby permitting the eye to go forward more rapidly.

3. The eye is helped to sweep constantly forward. A poor reader looks back and forth across a line of type or up and down across several lines aimlessly, letting his eyes fall where they will. As a result, he cannot follow the flow of thought which the author has conveyed.

One other habit which sometimes makes reading inefficient is that of linking it to some bodily motion other than that of the eyes. Perhaps, as a child, a man got the habit of saying words to himself as he read them and has never lost it. Since reading is very much faster than speaking, his speed of reading is greatly diminished. He may not even move his lips, but, without his knowing it, there will be movement in his vocal chords.

The modern techniques of reading improvement are based on the foregoing factors, as well as on others too complex to mention here. Many people "learned how to read" in school, but after a certain point gave up trying to improve their ability and therefore remained at a level far less than that which they could achieve. (Do you remember Dr. Book's point that when effort stops, so does the refinement of one's skills?) Other people had some limitation, perhaps poor eyes or poor teaching or an environment without much reading material to give them constant and varied practice. Therefore, they bogged down. Now when they need the skill, they do not have it. Often they are not even aware of that fact.

Normal readers, as well as poor ones, can profit from reading instruction. Paul Witty [8], after reviewing the research, concluded:

> It is possible for almost any adult to improve his reading both in rate and in comprehension. In practice, most of us adopt a congenial pace in reading, much below our actual capacity. And some of us read everything in the same way—a newspaper, a novel, or a conference report. In many cases, this is a snail's pace; in others it is a relatively slow rate that becomes habitual. There are, of course, large numbers of adults who read various types of material skillfully. Yet many of these people can improve their reading habits.

You may want to consider the possibility of concentrating for a while on improving your competence in reading, turning aside for a time from other learning purposes. If by this you can greatly increase your ability to understand what you read as well as your ability to read more rapidly, you will be ahead in the long run. Generally speaking, you should concentrate on reading improvement under these circumstances:

1. When you feel that your study is seriously blocked by slowness in reading, inability to comprehend what you read, or awareness that you are reading everything in the same way.

2. When you resume serious study after long absence from it. By "serious" study is meant any long or hard undertaking, such as a degree program at a university or a decision that for the rest of your life you want always to be engaged in study.

3. When you find it easy and convenient to undertake a reading improvement program. You may have excellent facilities for doing so immediately available. Such a program will deepen your understanding of your own thought processes and open up countless vistas for you.

If possible, anybody who wishes to improve his reading competence should seek the specialized help of a reading center or clinic. Tens of thousands of adults do so every year at the centers now available throughout the country. They are usually staffed by trained and qualified professional workers who can help you diagnose and correct your own reading difficulties. Such centers provide social interaction with teachers and with other learners. Also, because you must proceed on a regular schedule, you are helped to stay on the path of progress.

In selecting a center, it is wise to choose one operated by an established educational institution, such as a university, college, public school system, or library. Some commercial reading centers are highly qualified and do outstanding work, but others are inadequate and cannot fulfill their promises. If no institutional center is available and you must use a commercial one, check up in advance on its standards, its reputation, and its fees.

If a reading center is not available, the next best procedure is to work your way carefully through a self-instruction book. There are several excellent ones on the market, written by directors of reading clinics or other specialists who can suggest general principles and exercises which are useful for everyone. Since such authors cannot diagnose your specific needs, a self-help book is not as good as a course at a center.

A generally useful book is the one by Leedy, which has already been cited. You will probably find several such books at your local public library, and you may wish to examine them to choose the one which seems best to you. If you plan to work your way systematically through it, however, you should own a copy so that you can write in it.

Under guidance, many adults can increase their speed of reading by from 75 per cent to 100 per cent on organized nonfiction material. If they start at a speed of 200 words a minute, for instance, they often end, six or eight weeks later, with a rate of 350 to 400 words, and with no loss of comprehension. Some adults can do even better than this, and others, of course, cannot do as well.

Some teachers make much bolder promises, saying that they can teach adults to read from 2,000 to 12,000 words per minute. Let us look at this claim with some realism. This present book has about 50,000 words. If you read it at the rate of 5,000 words per minute, you could get through it in ten minutes. You would need to turn over eighteen pages every minute, and your eye would need to sweep with lightning rapidity down each page. If you did that, how much do you think you would remember? To be sure, you would have the general idea of the book. But would you have absorbed the meaning of "Pied Beauty" in your single glance at it? Would you have pondered and finally chosen the most meaningful (to you) suggestion for establishing a schedule for study?

Do not put your faith in people who tell you they can increase your reading speed twenty or fifty or a hundred times. Would you believe anybody who told you such things about other skills? Do you think you could increase your typing speed from forty-five to nine hundred words a minute or learn to run a mile in twenty-four seconds instead of eight minutes?

The heart of reading is comprehension. Your speed should be only that which permits you to understand and enjoy each kind of material. The rate will therefore vary greatly. For easy, interesting, organized non-fiction, you may go at the rate of 450 words per minute. For poetry you may need twenty minutes to read the same number of words. For mathematics, you may need to spend three hours working out the formulas which occupy the same space as 450 words.

USING YOUR COMPETENCE TO FULLEST ADVANTAGE

The central message of this chapter is that reading is a vital and essential skill for everyone who wishes to learn. William S. Gray and Bernice Rogers [9] have studied a large number of adults and believe that the truly mature reader has these characteristics:

He is enthusiastic about reading and shows this fact by spending a great deal of time voluntarily pursuing this interest. He reads widely in a large number of subject-matter areas and does not merely skim each one lightly but explores it and tries to get at deeper levels of meaning. He is consciously aware of many different reasons for reading and actually pursues a large number of them. He reads many kinds of material but tends to choose that which has an intellectual challenge for him and conveys great richness of ideas. He has the ability to read difficult material and, in doing so, he can readily grasp its meaning and apply the ideas which he has gained.

Few reach this state of advanced "maturity," but it is a goal well worth trying to achieve. When we realize this fact, we understand the full meaning of a remark said to have been made by the great German author, Goethe: "The dear good people don't know how long it takes to learn to read. I've been at it eighty years and cannot say yet that I have reached the goal." He showed no sign of regretting the effort he had made.

Chapter 7

The Art of Writing

"Writing maketh an exact man," said Bacon—and his remark suggests both a promise and a problem. Ideas, notions, impressions, reflections, images, and observations float about the mind in all kinds of shifting patterns. Putting ideas down on paper is the best way to understand them clearly, to know precisely what one is talking about, and to fit various thoughts into a coherent whole. Once ideas are recorded properly, their meaning and pattern will be exact. But capturing and recording them: there's the problem!

It is never fully solved, even by the most gifted author. His ambitions always outreach his performance, even though he works at an advanced level and uses a technique perfected after much use. For most adults the difficulty about writing is that they have forgotten that it is a skill—an advanced and complex skill, to be sure, but a skill nonetheless. The writer, like the golfer or the diver, must keep in practice if he wishes to continue to perform successfully.

Because writing is so important in achieving a clear viewpoint and exactness of expression, it is an essential part of most serious kinds of study, whether undertaken individually or as an assignment in a course. The purpose of this chapter is to suggest certain ways to improve one's skill in writing of the sort

107

usually carried out as part of a study program—what was earlier called "organized nonfiction." Each of the many other kinds of writing, such as poems, novels, letters, or short stories, has its own requirements which must be met but which cannot be dealt with here.

SOME GENERAL RULES

Four general rules are basic to all good writing. The failure to observe them causes many people to write poorly.

1. Know what you are trying to achieve. You may be writing a paper assigned in a course and therefore think that you already know what its purpose should be. But pause for a moment and think more deeply. What is it that the instructor really wants? More important, what do you want to say?

There are at least five different kinds of papers, though none is precisely and sharply separated from the others. The *explanatory* paper is an effort to report accurately on some subject that is known directly to the author or that is described or explained to him by others. The *experience* paper describes an event or series of events in the writer's life or in that of someone else. The *opinion* paper reports judgments about things; it reveals the opinions of the author. The *reference* paper is a review and appraisal of the literature dealing with some subject. The *research* paper presents the results of a basic investigation made by the author.

Since each of these five types determines the organization and method of approach you should use, it is wise to decide in advance what kind of a paper you plan to write. Do you need to do independent research, or will a paper drawn from library sources be more appropriate? How much can you rely on your own personal experience? Is accurate reporting or explanation your sole aim, or do you also wish to interpret— or even to argue? Such questions as these are so basic that you must answer them before you construct even the first plan of the paper you propose to write.

A paper may, to be sure, contain several elements. You may want to start with a personal anecdote to gain interest, go on to a description based on your own knowledge, broaden out to include library sources, extend the coverage still further to report on an independent investigation, and, finally, end with a statement of your own opinion. If such is the case, then each section will have its own purpose and each must be written differently. (For example, it would be highly inappropriate to insert personal opinions and judgments into the description of your research.) Your organization and your approach is determined by the fact that you have a complex rather than a simple purpose.

2. Decide what *you* have to say. Any piece of writing, whether it fits into any one of the five kinds or is some combination of them, gets part of its meaning because you are writing it. What do you know that is different from general knowledge and should therefore be explained? What experiences or opinions flow from your own background? Even if you are writing a reference or research paper, what problem do you choose to study or what approach do you use? Nobody else is exactly like you, and your paper should reveal that you have recognized that fact and taken advantage of it.

3. Think always of the person or persons for whom you are writing. The process of getting your ideas or your story down on paper is important, but the purpose of writing is almost always to communicate. You want to instruct, to interest, to amuse, or to persuade your reader or readers. Therefore, you must both get your message down and get it across.

Sometimes these latter two purposes must be worked out separately. You may need, first of all, to record what you want to say—clearly, completely, correctly, and briefly. Even while you do so, you will be aware of your probable audience, and that fact will either consciously or subconsciously influence what you set down. Then, when you have your ideas on paper, you will need to think more directly about the person or persons for whom you are writing. Is it a teacher? If so, write for him. Is it a group of people? If so, what are they like? Is it for publication? If so, what kinds of people are reached by the publication you want to use? Is it initially for a person or a group but ultimately for a wider audience? Then write for the immediate purpose but have in mind the people you want to reach eventually.

As you keep on writing, you will gradually learn to think simultaneously about what you want to say and the audience you want to reach. Even when you have reached this level, however, the final step in writing each paper is to think back over it to be sure that, at every point, it adequately answers two questions: Have I said exactly what I want to say? Have I said it in the right way to communicate to my target audience?

4. Have the necessary tools at hand: pencil, pen, ink, typewriter, paper, carbon paper, eraser, a dictating machine. Depending upon your writing habits, you will need some or all of these, but you should also have the other tools a writer needs: reference books.

The one essential item is a dictionary. There are many available, and they vary greatly in quality and scope, from a simple, brief, paperback volume with bare definitions to the magnificent, many-volumed *Oxford English Dictionary*. (If you have never seen the complete *OED*, as scholars call it, browse through it the next time you are in a good library; you will discover the set to be a revelation of the depth of your language.) Whatever dictionary you possess, use it to find the correct meaning and spelling of words. If you have no other source, it can also help increase your richness of vocabulary.

The second most important resource is a thesaurus, which gives many ways of expressing various ideas and helps you find the right word to convey the exact nuance of meaning. There are two kinds of thesaurus. In the first, whose basic arrangement is alphabetical, you simply look up the word which comes closest to the one you want, and there you will find many other terms and expressions which are similar to it, though each one has its own particular shade of meaning. In the second kind of thesaurus, you first look up the word in the alphabetical index which then refers you to the main part of the book, which is organized in terms of basic ideas. Either thesaurus is satisfactory, and you will be surprised how often you use one once you get the habit.

The other reference works most often needed for your writing (as well as for your other ways of getting an education) are a dictionary of quotations, a book (such as Fowler's *Modern English Usage*) that explains the rules for using words and expressions, and an encyclopedia. You will find different versions of all three at your public library, and most good bookstores have the first two. At either place, you can compare the various editions and decide which ones seem most suitable for you.

READ. THINK. WRITE. LET IT REST. RETHINK. REWRITE.

The six steps chosen for the heading of this section were suggested by one woman when she was asked how she wrote papers. Again and again, successful adult students said that they used the same basic process. Here it is, spelled out in detail.

1. Start as soon as possible after you have received an assignment for a paper or have decided to write one. In some ways, this step is the hardest, for the labor of writing is easy to postpone. You will not have time for the later steps, however, unless you first follow this one.

2. Sketch out your paper using rules 1, 2, and 3 in the preceding section, Some General Rules. You may simply reflect about these three matters if you wish to do so, but it is much better to make notes about them. These notes do not need to be precisely written. The main thing is to get down on paper what you want to do, what you want to say, and the person or persons for whom you are writing.

3. List all the ideas you want to include in your paper. Do not worry about logic at this point, and do not bother to develop your ideas fully. As time goes on, keep adding ideas to this list as they occur to you.

4. Do any reading you have to do. As you read, make careful notes. Some people use cards of various sizes, but, in the long run, it is probably best to use ordinary-sized sheets of paper. Use one sheet or one card for each idea, being sure to identify its source. When you take notes from a particular book or article, read it all the way through first; then go back to take your notes. In this way, you can choose the best quotations or find the best ways to summarize what the author says. If you copy anything, *be sure you do so exactly*. Put the complete reference to the article or book at the end of each note. (For example, don't just give a source as "Holmes." Which Holmes? Which book or article of his? What page? If you are not exact, you may have to spend many tedious hours later on trying to locate the quotation you want to use or cite.) On any given subject far more has usually been written than you can

possibly read, so choose only the references that seem most meaningful for your needs.

5. Outline the paper as you want to write it. This step is so important that it will be the subject of the next part of this chapter.

6. Write your first draft. You might follow the practice of one student: "I simply write, and keep writing, until I feel I have exhausted the subject." Later in this chapter are some suggestions to follow if you have trouble at this stage.

7. Rewrite your first draft. Here is what one man does: "I cut down drastically and tighten it up, picking and choosing the most important parts. I take my usable material and work it over until I feel satisfied. I find that it is always better to have more than you need, and the experience of cutting and tightening is a useful one."

8. Put your revised draft aside for at least a few days, preferably for as much time as you can. You will find that you come back to it with a remarkably fresh approach. You can now look in a detached fashion at what you have written, correct its weaknesses, and strengthen its good points.

Sometimes it helps to have other people read your papers and make comments on them. This practice is a good one if the person concerned is a sympathetic and constructive critic who wants to help you. Even so, it is usually wise not to let anyone else read your material until you have had a chance to make it as good as you can. One purpose in writing is to aid your powers of expression, and you will best do so if you learn to be constantly and constructively critical of your own work. Your confidence in what you have written may be destroyed if you show it to someone too early, before you have had a chance to find and correct its weaknesses yourself.

If you have difficulty in looking at your own work

objectively, you might have someone else read it aloud to you. If *you* read it aloud, you merely reinforce your own familiarity with it. If someone else reads it, you hear it with a freshness not otherwise possible.

WORKING FROM OR TO AN OUTLINE

The logical way to write is to think about your purpose, your audience, and your ideas, and, in the light of all three, to set down an outline which indicates the order in which you plan to present what you want to say. If you can do it that way, fine! Go right ahead! But many people have difficulty at this point. Therefore, this section will deal, first, with the logical method of approach and then go on to suggest two other approaches which may be necessary if the "right" way doesn't work for you.

1. Ideas must always be presented to the reader in some order—and that order is dictated basically by what is to be said. If you are writing a historical account, you may use a time sequence: what happened first, what happened next, and so on. If you are dealing with the steps in a procedure (as was the case in the last section), your organization is in terms of the steps themselves. Among other common possibilities are these: alphabetical order, order of importance, numerical order, geographical order, and simple-to-complex order.

If your paper is long or complicated, you will need to use several different orders. Suppose you are dealing with the history of three British colonies in West Africa: Nigeria, Gold Coast (now Ghana), and Sierra Leone. You might use a basically historical order by dividing your paper into periods. Then each period could be divided into a general account and an analysis

of developments in each country. Your broad outline
would then look something like this:

I. Early history of the three colonies before British
colonization
   A. General characteristics
   B. Nigeria
   C. Gold Coast
   D. Sierra Leone

II. Rise and decline of British colonial influence
   A. General characteristics
   B. Nigeria
   C. Gold Coast
   D. Sierra Leone

III. Coming of independence
   A. General characteristics
   B. Ghana
   C. Nigeria
   D. Sierra Leone

Under each section, you would then need to find some
principle of organization to put logic and order into
the material you want to present. You might, for example, be sure to include in each one a separate treat-
ment of political, economic, and social factors.

The foregoing outline is not the only one possible.
You could organize your material basically in terms of
countries, using the historical periods as subheads. Or
you could deal with such topics as political history, economic history, and social history, with a further break-
down in terms of country or historical period or both.
In any case, don't be too mechanical or too arbitrary.
You may have some material on Nigeria which you
wish to include, though you do not have comparable
facts for the other two countries. In that case, you
would want to change your outline to fit your material,
not force your material to fit the outline.

In addition to the basic outline, which usually deals
with the major, middle part of a paper, you will also

need to add a beginning and an end. Readers expect to be introduced to the subject in an interesting fashion and to be told what is coming in later pages. At the end, they want to have a suitable conclusion which rounds out the paper and makes it into a complete and artistic whole. If you look at articles in magazines, you will see how skillfully professional writers prepare not only their basic messages but also the beginnings and the conclusions of their papers.

2. Suppose that a suitable outline does not come to your mind. All kinds of ideas and topics whirl around in your head and your attention flits from one to the other. No standard order seems to be appropriate. You just can't get started. What should you do?

The best way out of this difficulty is to start listing on a sheet of paper all the possible topics you might include. Let them pour forth with no order at all, just as they come to your mind. A trivial item may be followed by a major one and that in turn by a simple illustration. Put down in each case just enough to record the idea. Don't bother developing it or even stating it in a complete sentence. Just get it down. If need be, move on to a second sheet and a third.

Presently, your pencil will begin to slow down. There really weren't as many ideas in that whirl as you had thought. Now that they are down on paper and no longer all jumbled up in your mind, you can look at them more clearly. Usually a method of organizing the topics will flash into your mind. You will see that they can all be usefully grouped under four main headings—or three, or five.

At that point, spread out on your desk as many fresh sheets of paper as you have proposed headings. At the top of each, put the central idea for that major heading. It is best to state each idea as a complete sentence, for this practice gives your thoughts greater precision and clarity. Then go down your first jumbled list and copy each item onto the sheet with the appropriate heading. Here also it may be useful to state each such item in a complete sentence.

Your first organization may need to be revised several times to take account of new thoughts, a clearer viewpoint, or additional data. Ordinarily, however, these revisions are not as difficult as the establishment of a first basic organization and often are merely refinements of it.

The process of establishing the basic organization of your material may already have given you the necessary beginning and conclusion of the paper. If not, you will want to add them. But now it is easier to do so because now you know what you want to say. If, by chance, the beginning and the ending sections simply do not occur to you, proceed to write the body of the paper. Somewhere along the way, a suitable introduction and conclusion will present themselves.

3. Another technique for developing an outline may be useful when you have just a few ideas and do not yet see how you are going to get others to develop into an entire paper. In this case, perhaps the best process is to write out each idea just as though you were preparing it for the final paper. Doing so will stimulate you to think of other ideas. Write them out, too! Put each paragraph or section on a separate sheet of paper. After a while you may well find that you have accumulated a fairly large body of material. Look over it and, as you do so, add any additional ideas you may have. Presently you will find the organization coming into your mind. Then it is a fairly easy task to divide up your already-written sections into piles and begin to weave your existing material into a logical and coherent whole.

Be sure that it *is* logical and coherent! Some of the passages you have written just won't fit. Throw them out—or put them into a miscellaneous folder for possible use in another paper. Other paragraphs have followed a discarded approach, are written in the wrong tense, or are now reversed in their structure. Rewrite them so that they fit into the new pattern.

This third technique is not as good as the first two, chiefly because it requires you to do so much rewriting, but if it is the only way you can get your mind clear and get down to work on the paper, use it!

WRITING—AND REWRITING

Writing is both a means of communication and an art form. The outline of a paper should be transformed into a series of clear, coherent paragraphs following one another in logical order and conveying your meaning to your audience. Your central aim should be clarity, correctness, and completeness. Throughout this process you will say things in your own individual way, for no two people write in exactly the same fashion. But you will almost always find that the first way you write is not the best. It is in the process of revision that you sharpen your sentences, enrich your ideas, and make your whole presentation more skillful.

Everybody must teach himself to write. You can secure advice, criticism, and help from others. You can enlarge your understanding by studying books on composition. You can study examples of successful writing to see how the authors achieve their effects. But these are all accessory aids. The central idea is to keep everlastingly at your writing. Epictetus [1], the ancient Roman, put the matter correctly when he said: "If you would be a writer, write!"

This section, therefore, has only a limited aim. It presents some of the special techniques adult students have learned to use in helping themselves to write more efficiently and well.

1. Write your paper all the way through so that you have the satisfaction of a complete first draft. Then, and only then, can you see the whole body of content objectively. At that point, begin your rewriting.

2. Do not follow your outline slavishly. In the very process of writing, ideas become clearer and change their relative importance. As these changes occur, move away from your original outline toward one closer to your later and more advanced ideas. Be sure that in the process of rewriting, however, you maintain balance and perspective. Don't let your enthusiasm for some particular topic lead you to give it too much weight.

3. If you are having trouble writing what you want to say, look ahead in your outline until you find a topic which you *can* write about. Write it. Then find another such topic and deal with it. Presently you will find you can go back to tackle the difficult section confidently. It often happens that the first paragraph or section of a paper is the last one to be written. Of course, when you write things out of context, you will need to revise them when you put them together in your final draft.

4. Never stop writing at "a good stopping place." Instead, if you see your way clear to the end of a section, stop before you get to it. Then, knowing exactly what to write when you start the next day, you can beat that great hazard of all writers: getting started. An even better use of this principle is to go on to the end of a section but not to stop there. Think ahead about the next section and know just how you are going to start when you sit down again to write. Then when you come to your desk, you will be prepared to go to work at once.

5. Write as close to final copy as you can. Do not simply sketch in ideas with the notion that you will develop them later. Put them down now. You will have more ideas later. If you use references, put the citations to them in the correct form from the very beginning.

You will save a great deal of time later on. It usually happens that you must revise and rewrite and that your first draft won't turn out to be your final copy. That final version will, however, be very much better if from the start you have tried to make it as good as you can.

6. As you rewrite, try to use several different approaches. Normally, when you first return to a paper after having let it "sit" for several days, you find all kinds of ways to make it better. Presently, however, you slow down. That is the time (if you are really striving for improvement) to examine the paper from different angles. Here are some questions you might ask yourself:

Does the whole organization hang together?

Is the beginning really interesting?

Have I brought the paper to a successful close?

Have I used words which best convey my meaning, avoiding repetition, triteness, or inexactness?

Does what I say sound natural and fresh, not stilted or labored?

Have I polished each sentence so that it says forcefully and well just what I want it to say?

Are my paragraphs well constructed, with a clear well-developed idea in each one?

Are my sentences varied so that short ones and long ones are woven together for a pleasing effect?

Does each paragraph flow naturally from the one before it, or are there awkward breaks in thought?

What are still the weak parts of the paper and how can I improve them?

IF YOU ARE REALLY SERIOUS

In this chapter so far, writing has been treated as a normal part of the learning process, the necessary aid to many kinds of study. The improvement of the ability to express oneself exactly should be a goal sought by everyone, and writing is the best means to that end.

In two special situations, however, it may be necessary to pay particular attention to writing skill. The first is when one feels particularly inadequate and in need of special help. The other is when one feels he has a particular talent for writing and wants to improve his ability to a very high level.

If you believe that writing is one of your weak points, there are four things you might do.

1. The best plan is to take a course in English composition, if you can find one which meets your particular needs. The need for improved writing skills is so widely recognized in our society that most adult educational institutions have one or more courses in this subject. Often these courses are offered at several different levels of competence, one of which may be appropriate for you. In a class, you receive the special help of a teacher, and you also gain from the shared experience of working with others who have the same problems as yourself. Do not sign up for an English course, however, unless you have explored it fully enough to know that it is at the right level for you.

2. If you find it difficult or inconvenient to take a class with others, you can take one by correspondence. Many state universities offer such programs at fairly low cost, and the extension division of your own institution will send you a catalog or tell you where to write to get one.

3. You can hire a tutor who can help you improve your skills. This method is the most expensive, but it is also the most personalized, and therefore most likely to fit your own needs. If you do not know of any person who can help you, you can consult the principal of the high school or the head of the English department at a nearby college or community college.

4. You can work your way through a textbook on

composition, studying its basic principles and trying to put them into effect in your writing. There are many such books; if possible, you ought to look through the ones available in your local bookstore or library. One of the most widely used is Porter Perrin's *Writer's Guide and Index to English* [2].

Even if you feel that your talents place you at the upper end of the scale of writing ability, you may find it useful to follow one of these four suggestions. You would, of course, take advanced composition courses rather than elementary ones, and your tutor would work with you at an entirely different level. But even writers at advanced levels can still learn a great deal by going through such books as that by Perrin and particularly by using the index which makes up the second half of his book. Going beyond this elementary work, the prospective author will find an array of others, all the way from simple manuals of particular techniques, such as Rudolf Flesch's *The Art of Readable Writing* [3], to very advanced books, such as Arthur Quiller-Couch's *On the Art of Writing* [4]. Writers love to write about writing—and other writers love to read what they have written. You will find no lack of books to give you advice.

Another way to improve is to strive to equal an established writer. Many authors have used the means of direct imitation to teach themselves to write. Robert Louis Stevenson was one and Benjamin Franklin [5] was another. Here is how Franklin did it, in his own words:

> About this time I met with an odd volume of the *Spectator* . . . I thought the writing excellent, and wished, if possible, to imitate it. With this view I took some of the papers, and making short hints of the sentiment in each sentence, laid them by a few days, and then, without looking at the book,

tried to complete the papers again, by expressing each hinted sentiment at length, and as fully as it had been expressed before, in any suitable words that should come to hand. Then I compared my *Spectator* with the original, discovered some of my faults, and corrected them. . . . I also sometimes jumbled my collections of hints into confusion, and after some weeks endeavored to reduce them into the best order, before I began to . . . complete the paper. This was to teach me method in the arrangement of thoughts. By comparing my work afterwards with the original, I discovered many faults and amended them; but I sometimes had the pleasure of fancying that, in certain particulars of small import, I had been lucky enough to improve the method or the language, and this encouraged me to think I might possibly in time come to be a tolerable English writer, of which I was extremely ambitious.

But of all the advice for the budding author, that of Epictetus is still the best. Many people who feel the urge to be authors really want the satisfaction of having written without the labor of writing. They will never have that satisfaction.

CONCLUSION

The theme of this chapter was expressed in its opening words. The vague general conceptions of the mind cannot have precise form until one has written them down—and then refined them. The capacity to be exact and to know what you are talking about is one which is well worth having—but one for which it is necessary to work. Some of the pieces of writing which we read and admire seem so simple and direct that we can scarcely believe the labor to which the author has gone to make them so. But everyone who has ever tried to write well will agree with Alexander Pope [6] :

> True Ease in Writing comes from Art, not Chance,
> As those move easiest who have learn'd to dance.

Chapter 8

Shared Learning

Of all the ways by which adults learn, classes and groups are most familiar, for these are the customary patterns of education throughout childhood and youth. Here as elsewhere, familiarity sometimes leads to contempt. Many men and women act as though they believe that when they were young, they should learn in classrooms, but now that they are grown up, they should learn only by themselves.

As soon as this idea is examined, however, it begins to appear ridiculous. Where is the youth of twenty-two who is so wise that he will never again need anyone to guide his learning? (Ben Jonson [1] put the matter very sharply: "Hee that was onely taught by himselfe had a foole to his Master.") Who can keep his mind sharp and active all his life without whetting it against the minds of others? Who can make his full contribution to the community without learning how to be an effective member and leader of organizations? Who has so many congenial friends who share his intellectual interests that he does not need to discover others? Who does not need to have his vision enlarged by the exposure to wholly new viewpoints which he would never find by himself?

In any given year, you may not want to take a class or join a group, but if you stay away too long from shared learning experiences, you will find that your mind begins to lose its keenness and your horizon gradually closes in. People learn together in many kinds of groups. This chapter deals with three of the major types. The most familiar form is the *class*, with a teacher who knows the content and guides the learning. The second is the *organized group*, with no formal teacher but with a well-established program under some kind of overall guidance. The third is the *independent group*, organized by people who take the initiative to get together to learn in some fashion. Each of these three will be dealt with in turn.

HOW TO PROFIT FROM EACH MEETING OF A CLASS

A code of customary behavior grows up for all of the usual ways in which people get together. Anybody going to a party, for example, tries to dress appropriately, to get there at the proper time, and to behave in a manner suitable for that particular affair. In these ways, he not only does what he knows is expected but also gets the most out of the occasion for himself, even though the only purpose is fun.

In almost any kind of group learning situation, and particularly in a classroom, there are appropriate ways of behaving. Most people have a general awareness of what is expected of them, but only accomplished students realize how much their learning is aided by what they do at each session. These are some of the most important guides to action:

1. Prepare yourself psychologically for each session. Think about the end of the last meeting and how this new one will probably follow it. Reflect about the content to be covered. Have your background reading com-

pleted. If you are not ready when the class starts, you may waste ten or fifteen minutes while you gradually get warmed up to the topic under discussion. Often those are the most important minutes, for many lecturers give their basic viewpoints at the start and then spend the rest of the time elaborating them.

2. Go to every session. It is all too easy sometimes to skip a class. Adults are busy and emergencies come up. Then, too, the subject may not be too interesting at the moment. But the missing of one class is likely to lead to the missing of the rest of them. Students who stick through sessions which are not too interesting to them often find that it is just those sessions, looked at later, which prove to be the most significant. If you decide that a class is really not for you, then stop it and take another. Do not slip into a pattern of missed classes, for in this way you unconsciously make the decision not to continue, and you usually have a guilty feeling about doing so.

3. Get to the classroom early enough so that you can get settled before the session starts. If possible, arrive early enough so that you can visit with other early arrivers, including the instructor.

4. Choose a place to sit which is desirable as far as seeing and hearing are concerned and which avoids distractions. In most classrooms, this seat is in the center toward the front of the room, and without a view out the window or the open door. Try not to sit next to a talkative neighbor; if you must, indicate by your manner that you are trying hard to concentrate on what the instructor is saying or on what the group is doing.

5. Get all your assigned work in when it is due. The instructor must plan his time, and it is an inconvenience to him to have papers come in late. Even more important, the failure to do your work at the proper time leads you into the habit of delay.

6. Do more work than the minimum required. Do

not parade your extra knowledge (adults dislike show-offs just as much as children do), but if you can make easy and natural use of it in class discussion, do not hesitate to do so. Part of the value of adult education lies in the shared experience and knowledge of those who take part.

7. Concentrate on what is happening, and show by your manner that you are doing so. This last part can be overdone. The overeager lady who sits with an exalted expression drinking in every word is an object of ridicule; we suspect that she is posing. The best practice is to sit comfortably but alertly, focusing your thoughts on what is happening. Sometimes it is hard to hold your attention firmly fixed, particularly if you haven't been taking courses for a long time. Note-taking helps in this process. So does a conscious effort to interact with the mind of the instructor by mentally phrasing questions, seeking illustrations, and probing for the basic structure of what he is saying. You may need to start by concentrating for only ten minutes or so, gradually building up the length of time as you gain the power to do so.

8. Don't engage in private conversations during a class or anticipate the end of the period by beginning to stack up papers and books, putting away equipment, or showing in any other fashion that you are getting ready to go. To do either not only is rude to the instructor and your fellow group members but also signals the fact that you have turned your attention away from the class itself. It is precisely at this point that you may miss something crucial.

9. Don't hurry away from class unless you absolutely must. It is often pleasant and rewarding to wind up your stay in leisurely fashion, having a chat with one or more of your classmates or with the instructor.

10. As soon as possible after the class, review its contents. One way to do so is by writing up your notes;

another is to think over the major points while riding
or walking home. Whatever the method, an immediate
review will help you to understand and remember.

UNDERSTANDING THE ESSENCE
OF A LECTURE

The lecture is the most widely criticized but the most
widely used method of teaching. It is like the little girl
with the curl: it may be very, very good, or it may be
horrid. At its best, it is an absorbing revelation of pro-
found knowledge presented by an exciting personality.
At its worst, it is a droning repetition of material already available in a textbook.

Adults have more choice than young people as far as
taking classes and listening to lectures are concerned.
If the material is too dull to be tolerated, adults can
declare their independence by dropping the course. (If
so, they should not hesitate to give their reason to the
counselor or the director of the program. Everybody
will gain as a result, particularly the lecturer who is
thereby challenged to improve his method of teaching.)
Sometimes, however, adults are trapped into taking dull
courses because of a need to complete degree requirements or because participation has been "encouraged"
by an employer. If so, each lecture session should be
made as creative an experience as possible.

Usually the situation is far better than the last paragraph suggests. Most lecturers have been stimulated or
forced by their students to be effective. A teacher does
not last very long in the free air of adult education if
he cannot teach. Even so, every lecturer is different,
and therefore it is necessary to adapt yourself to each
one (good or bad) before you can get the essence of
what he has to say.

You will be greatly aided by the fact that the relationship between teacher and student is different in adult classes than it is in classes for children and young people. Your instructor has no general authority over you, but only as much as he can win by his expertness. He is very often younger than you, but this fact presents no problem. Many adults like to have young instructors. Moreover, you can usually understand and appraise your teacher as a person in a way that a child never can. You see his strengths and his insecurities, his graces and his awkwardnesses. Sometimes by being tactful, you can help smooth the way for him when he gets into a bit of trouble. You may even make a personal friend of him, though you must be careful not to seem to take advantage of that fact, particularly if he is young and a bit unsure of his authority.

Listening to a lecture is in some ways like reading a book, but basically the two are separate skills. Both require the active use of the mind. In reading, however, you determine your own rate of speed; you decide when and where you will read, and you can go back and forth over the material as frequently as you wish. In a lecture, control is taken out of your hands and put into those of the lecturer. He sets the pace, and he covers his material but once. To compensate for these drawbacks, you do have the advantage of being able to ask him questions and get his help on your particular problems. Also, his material should be fresher and newer than that found in any book, and he can often relate it closely to your individual purposes.

Many of the earlier suggestions about classroom conduct will help you to profit from lectures. Here are a few additional points:

1. Adapt your style of listening to the characteristics of the particular lecturer. If he is a clear, concise speaker whose material shows a well-thought-out structure, devote your major attention to getting that structure into your own mind. If he is a stylist who makes his points gracefully but subtly, enjoy what he says,

but still try to get the essence of his ideas. If his talk is impressionistic and disconnected, capture the flashes of insight, but expect to get the basic structure from the text or some other source. If he encourages or permits questions, ask them, particularly if he is obscure, boring, or off the subject. In every case, try to have your mind interact with his to get the greatest value he can give you. Don't have an idealized conception of a lecturer and then criticize him because he does not live up to it. He may have an idealized conception of a student—and you may fall far short of it!

2. Learn to take notes and listen at the same time. Some people have no difficulty with this problem; others need to train themselves to let their minds work on two levels at once. On one, they are capturing on paper the essence of what has been said. On the other, they are listening for the new points. The only way to acquire this dual skill is by continued practice.

3. Listen carefully to discover what cues the lecturer gives you about his structure and his major points. Some speakers are perfectly clear in this respect. They announce that they are going to make five points; then they make them, one after the other, clearly labeling each; and finally they review all five, perhaps identifying those they think are most significant. Not all subject matter lends itself to this kind of presentation, however, and not all lecturers use it who might do so. But usually if you come to know the habits of the speaker, you can find out that he has certain key words that suggest what is important to him, or he clearly signals the transitions between one topic and another.

4. Record in your notes some of the speaker's illustrations and anecdotes as well as his major points. In Marcel Proust's great novel *Remembrance of Things Past*, the leading figure finds that the taste of a cookie dipped in tea reminds him of his aunt and brings back to him a flood of memories. You can use this principle in remembering the points in a lecture. Do not merely

capture the bare bones of the outline. Put in some of the lecturer's unusually effective illustrations or sentences. Two months later, you may find that the illustration gives you a richer memory of the subject than does the statement of the principle.

5. Record any basic idea which seems strange to you or with which you do not agree. Everyone tends to suppress or underestimate facts or notions which do not fit into his predetermined pattern of belief. You need to guard against forgetting ideas you should remember just because you find them strange or disagreeable.

6. Strike a balance between too much and too little in taking class notes. There is no point in capturing everything the instructor says, word for word; you would have too much material to review. Anyway, most lectures have only a few major points which deserve to be remembered. Moreover, if you write a great deal, you are likely to be so busy "getting it all down" that you don't have it in the only place that really counts—your mind. If you take too few notes, on the other hand, you are likely to find them sketchy and meaningless later on.

SHARING IN THE DISCUSSION

In most classes, time is allowed for discussion or for asking questions. Such activity is, in fact, often more rewarding with adults than with young people, for men and women have backgrounds of experience which they can share and which often make the subject matter deeply meaningful.

A few experienced adult students, on thinking the matter over however, have decided that they get more when they do not participate. One man observed:

> I have discovered that class sessions are more rewarding to me when I keep my mouth closed. If the instructor directs a question to the class, I

know the answer approximately eight times out of ten, but what will it benefit me if I answer? So I listen, and usually someone else knows the answer too and volunteers an answer with perhaps a slightly different twist or different emphasis, and after he has answered, I know more than I would had I been the one to answer. I realize that should everyone do this, there wouldn't be any classroom response, but since I am primarily interested in my own increase in knowledge, and since there has been no shortage of students willing to show how bright they are, there seems no immediate danger.

One must respect such a thoughtful viewpoint, though it is in the minority. Most men and women who take classes believe that they gain greatly from personal participation. "The more I participate the more I learn," said one of them, and his comments have been echoed countless times. Research has shown fairly conclusively that the college students who take part most frequently and effectively get the highest grades. Though adults may not be working for grades, it seems likely that they will learn much more if they share actively in the discussion.

Why don't more of them do so? L. A. Kirkendall [2], in a study made with young people, found that lack of participation comes from feeling poorly prepared, from timidity, from a dislike of exposing one's ignorance, and from a fear of ridicule. These are precisely the reasons often given by adults.

The skillful teacher will create a situation in which there is a sympathetic attention to everyone's views and an encouragement of complete participation. In fact, many teachers think they have failed when they cannot get everyone to share in the discussion. Whether the teacher is sympathetic or not, you must be concerned with your own education. You must not let doubts and fears hold you back.

Do not be fooled by the seeming erudition of a

few students. They may not really be more learned than you but merely know some jargon which sounds impressive. Your view, expressed in your own words, may have more directness and freshness than they can manage. In any class, there are likely to be many people who are no more sure of themselves than you are of yourself. Your comment or question may have a greater response than you think it will. Also, you may encourage some of them to respond, and this fact will eventually benefit you.

Start participating early in the course, before the patterns of the class are set. If you don't, others may take over a dominant role, and you will feel more and more awkward as time goes on. The longer you stay out of the discussion, the more likely you are never to be able to share in it.

Never ask a fake question or participate solely for the sake of participation. Ask for an application of a general point you do not understand fully. Suggest such an application yourself and ask if you are right. Ask the teacher or another student to say a little more on some subject because you find it interesting. Use any of the other usual ways of asking or commenting, but always ask only about something for which you have a genuine concern.

Try to make any comment simply, in a friendly fashion. If any comment of yours does arouse laughter, join in it with the rest of the class.

One very successful student put the whole matter very briefly and eloquently:

> Always come to a session armed not only with the shield of the correct answers but also with the sword of one or two carefully thought out (and genuinely pertinent) questions. And many students would also do well to obtain the helmet of darkness and silence!

This last sentence suggests a fact which everyone knows: some people who participate in a class do so in a highly irritating fashion. Francis P. Robinson [3] has confirmed experimentally what most people sense: that the students in a college class tend to fall into three types, the disturbers, the quiet unknowns, and the leaders. These three are also found in adult classes. Sometimes the disturbers can be very disturbing indeed. Listen to one man sound off:

> I resent paying good money for a course wherein I expect to learn something and find the class time taken up with irrelevant questions and even dreary monologues from the inevitable class "taker overs." Class discussion is necessary for a true exchange of ideas, but when it strays far afield and goes into outer space, I feel that I've been cheated, and my mind begins to wander to more practical subjects like firearms and poison!

Benjamin Franklin [4], whom we found in the last chapter learning how to write, also had to learn how to discuss. He was, progressively, one kind of a disturber and then another before he finally became an effective participant. In the beginning he used "abrupt contradiction and positive argumentation." Then he read some examples of the Socratic dialogues and became charmed with them.

"I found this method safest for myself," he said, "and very embarrassing to those against whom I used it: Therefore I took a delight in it, practiced it continually, and grew very artful and expert in drawing people, even of superior knowledge, into concessions, the consequences of which they did not foresee, entangling them in difficulties out of which they could not extricate themselves, and so obtaining victories that neither myself nor my cause always deserved."

But gradually he came to see that he was doing the

wrong thing. He left this method, "retaining only the habit of expressing myself in terms of modest diffidence. . . . I wish well-meaning, sensible men would not lessen their power of doing good by a positive, assuming manner, that seldom fails to disgust, tends to create opposition, and to defeat every one of those purposes for which speech was given to us, to wit, giving or receiving information or pleasure."

Each member of a class or group should genuinely try to give or receive information and, if possible, pleasure. The teacher has chief responsibility for safeguarding the discussion and not letting the disturber take over. He needs help, however. Sometimes the members of a class must take matters into their own hands and show by their manner that they cannot tolerate disruptions. Sometimes they will perceive that the disturber of a class is a person who needs status, security, or friends—and will see if they can help solve his difficulty. Sometimes they will have to face up to the fact that a disturber is so serious a threat to class unity that they must ask the instructor to talk with him or perhaps even request him to leave the group.

By the way, it is always useful to ask yourself whether possibly you are a disturber. If you find yourself going on at length in a discussion, are you sure that everyone is listening to you with fascinated attention? If you are hotly pursuing a debate, are you really seeking the truth? If you keep on pressing a given line of questioning, are you certain that it is a matter of general concern?

COMING TO KNOW THE OTHER CLASS MEMBERS

One of the great advantages of learning in a class or group is that you can do so with people who not only have diverse backgrounds and approaches (which make them interesting) but also share similar interests with you and are usually congenial. This great value will not be achieved unless the class becomes a relaxed social group, the members of which are at ease with one another.

At the very minimum, the members of a class should know each other's names and general backgrounds. Going beyond this, they may well come to know one another as individuals. The obvious values of making new friends will then be reinforced by a greater spontaneity and interest in the classroom itself, with the result that each person learns more than he otherwise would. Out of such contacts can come extremely meaningful continuing relationships. One man, for example, commented:

> That first class happened to be just a terrific group of people. I've taken other similar things since, but I have never hit one where I found such a remarkable group of people. Only about fifteen or twenty, you know, if that many. Most of them were people whom I had never met before, though they lived in the community, and I formed some very good friends during that period. We had a habit after class, a bunch of us, of going over to a little restaurant nearby and having a soda and chatting, and as a result of that I got to know a half dozen people who are today my very best friends. And their interests, as you would gather from the fact that they were there, were in that direction, so I would begin to hear about things that I hadn't even considered or wasn't aware of, different kinds of activity, and I would get involved in this or that, not for social reasons but primarily because these people would communicate what they knew about these things and so I belonged.

Such an incident is not at all unusual. It happens every term in most adult educational centers.

The instructor can set a framework for this effective group spirit by being sure that everybody knows everybody else and by allowing plenty of time for participation. But some of the members of the group usually have to take an initiative in building a strong group spirit. Often they are surprised at how quickly their lead is followed by other members of the class.

JOINING AN ORGANIZED GROUP

Practically every foreign observer who has ever written about the United States has commented on our habit of forming and joining groups. In even very small towns, it is often incredible how many different organizations there are. Most of the leaders of almost any community will tell you it is "overorganized." When the matter is looked at more closely, however, it soon becomes apparent that a relatively small number of people carry most of the load of providing active membership and leadership in the various organizations.

Although many voluntary associations have purposes other than education, a large number list it as one of their functions or even as a central aim. Among them are the Red Cross, the PTA, the League of Women Voters, Rotary International, Kiwanis, Lions, the other service clubs, the Farm Bureau, and the many kinds of women's and garden clubs. People usually join such organizations from a variety of motives, of which the desire to learn is not always the major one.

Every such organization—no matter what its specific purpose may be—does much to educate its members not only in its area of special interest but also in the way in which a free and open society operates, with people joining and taking part in the associations of their own choice. Moreover, each person who accepts and discharges responsibilities learns something about leadership and how to exercise it.

Such groups are so varied that little can be said about them generally. If you are seeking to broaden your knowledge, however, you might find it congenial to do so through the medium of an organized group rather than in a class or by independent study. To gain the most from the experience, you need to follow four simple rules:

1. Believe firmly in the purpose of the organization.

2. Before you join, know exactly what is expected of you as a member.

3. Participate in the activities of the organization as fully as you can.

4. Be prepared to move into positions of leadership when you are asked to do so.

Another kind of organized group is that built entirely around the idea of education. Great books groups, home demonstration clubs, or parent education study circles are examples of this sort of activity. In these situations, a group of neighbors gets together to share in a special program worked out for their education. Sometimes they have helped to plan the program themselves; sometimes they have not. Usually there is no teacher, but there may be a leader who has been taught how to conduct a discussion. The group fits into some larger program guided and developed by highly trained experts. Therefore, it receives the advantage of skillful program making, but it is so organized that it can be carried out at little cost. Its structure is looser and more informal than that of a classroom, and the success of the venture depends on the capacity of the group to accept responsibility.

Such groups offer rapidly increasing opportunities for those who wish to further their education, and they often offer a novel and delightful experience. You might like to include one in your total learning program.

FORMING YOUR OWN GROUP

Throughout American society countless voluntary groups have come together because of individual initiative and have remained together because their members find satisfaction and enjoyment in what they learn. Nobody has any idea whether there are a hundred thousand or a million of these independent groups, nor are all their locations known but their great number and spread become apparent to anybody who seeks for examples.

The life span of such groups varies greatly. Some, such as the YMCA or Rotary, grow into worldwide movements; others never go beyond their own community but have a life span of a hundred years or more, though the membership changes a bit in the course of time! Still others, such as the Get-Together-and-Gab Club, die very soon.

The success of these groups is not, to be sure, wholly measurable by their length of life. A group may have great meaning for its members and yet last for only a fairly short time. Most independent groups probably do not survive for more than five to ten years, yet during that time they can be very educative for those who belong to them.

Despite much research, nobody knows all of the reasons why some groups have great significance for their members and others do not. The forces locked up in the small group seem to be almost as powerful and hard to analyze as the forces locked up in the atom. For anybody who is interested in starting an independent group for the purpose of learning, however, there are a few practical suggestions:

1. Be sure that you have explored the other possibilities of organized groups and classes. Some of them might be more congenial to you than a separate independent group.

2. Start with a small group of really interested people and expand slowly as you find you can absorb new members. You will know you are a real success when people start angling for invitations to join.

3. Have as diverse a membership as possible. This suggestion is not always easy to follow because one of the advantages of an independent group is that it can be built up of close neighbors, but neighbors tend to be so much alike that they soon run out of things to say to one another. Try to avoid this problem by inviting different kinds of people.

4. Keep the organization and the setting simple. Usually all you really need is a program chairman or a committee which can be selected each year. Meet in the most convenient place you can find, and if there are refreshments, make an absolute rule that they must be very simple, so that an unhealthy competition does not get started.

5. Have a definite plan of work or procedure. The members could prepare and give talks. The group could discuss books which everyone reads before coming to a meeting. The group might adopt some pre-planned program suggested by the extension division of your state university, your librarian, or the director of adult education in your local school system. Perhaps you will want to vary the program from year to year for the sake of diversity. But be sure that you have a well-worked-out and agreed-upon plan to guide your efforts.

6. Have a frank evaluation at least once a year, either by the whole group or by the program committee. Groups usually know how to correct their own problems if they are encouraged to do so and if those problems are discussed in a completely open manner.

7. Keep the group invigorated by new blood. People will move away, resign, or just stop coming—and rotation of membership is usually an advantage if va-

cancies are filled by new people with fresh ideas and viewpoints.

8. If the group really does go stale, agree not to meet for a year. Designate one person to check informally the following year and decide then whether the group ought to be brought back to life.

CONCLUSION

The last two chapters dealt with two parts of a quotation from Francis Bacon. In this chapter, we have considered the third and last. "Conference," he said, makes "a ready man." By "conferring" in any kind of group, one gains an ease and flexibility of approach both to subject matter and to other people which cannot be secured in any other way. We learn how to take part in the flashing interchange of ideas, to hold our own in debate and discussion, and to change our views as they need to be reshaped by greater knowledge. It is by these processes that we learn to be "ready."

Chapter 9

The Right Ways to Take Examinations

Suppose you were to visit a great European cathedral. As you approached, you would see it in its majesty, dominating the countryside. Then you would explore its separate parts: the altar, the nave, the transept, the chapels, the crypts, the cloister, the tower, the tapestries, the glass, and the carvings. As you looked carefully at each, you would be aware of its place in the total pattern of the cathedral. As you left, you would turn to look back. Once again you would see the cathedral as a whole, but now your knowledge would be far deeper and better organized than it was when you caught your first glimpse.

Mastering a complex body of subject matter may be likened to visiting a cathedral. You usually begin with a comprehensive but exterior view; you study the separate parts with the whole in mind; then, at the end, you look once again at the whole structure to bring it into a suitable perspective. As you prepare to be tested, the comprehensive review is your final look, and the examination is the way by which you, and your examiner, can judge how well you have understood the total pattern and all its parts.

Adults are used to meeting the tests that life constantly provides, and they know that success comes to those who have the necessary basic competence. This is true as well of those taking the formal examinations encountered in most learning programs; the best way to be sure of passing is to be a thorough master of the content. Most people do need help, however, in organizing and presenting their knowledge in order to gain the great learning advantages which come from comprehensive reviews and examinations. The purpose of this chapter is to suggest practical ways by which these processes may be made more profitable. Special emphasis will be given here to the final written examinations taken at the end of courses, since these are the ones which many adult students find most difficult. Many of the same general principles, however, apply to other tests and quizzes, including general and comprehensive examinations such as those that govern admission to the professions.

UNDERSTANDING THE PURPOSE OF AN EXAMINATION

Most adults like to test themselves—but they do not like to be tested. Editors of popular magazines learned long ago that their readers would respond positively to self-scoring examinations. Everybody likes to know how well he can perform and usually enjoys thoroughly any opportunity to judge his own capacities.

Most men and women, however, dislike taking examinations in courses. This process makes them feel they are returning to their school or college days, and old feelings of anxiety and inadequacy return. Children often do not understand the purpose of examinations, believing them to be ways by which the teacher finds out whether to reward or punish them. Since there is a certain amount of truth to this belief, it is hard to get it out of the child's mind. After a number of years, both the idea and the feelings it arouses become quite firmly fixed.

The basic purpose of an examination is to give a student and his teacher an estimate of how well they both have accomplished their purposes. The student wants to learn and the teacher wants to teach. A high grade on an examination gives a rough indication that they have both achieved their desires, while a low grade suggests that they have not.

MEASURING ACCOMPLISHMENT

Not all examinations are equally well constructed, but it may be useful to know what the teacher has in mind, or ought to have in mind, when he tries to measure accomplishment. Primarily, he is concerned about how well you have achieved the objectives of the course. If the aim is to have you grasp the broad sweep of American history and the facts which you must know in order to understand it, the examination should test for that understanding and that knowledge. If the aim is to help you know how to use the principles of grammar successfully, the examination must be of a different sort. Usually, the instructor has stated his course objectives in writing or orally (or they can be inferred from what he says), and you can get the best start in preparing for the examination by being sure that you have those objectives in mind. If he has not made them clear, examine the purposes stated in the textbook or try to think constructively about what they should be.

Second, the instructor selects from the material in the course those items he believes to be important and builds his examination around them. The student should always ask himself what the instructor thinks is of major significance, for the whole purpose of having a teacher is to take advantage of his guidance. You cannot always tell what he thinks important by what he stresses in class. He may feel that he is supplementing the material which you read or learn in other ways. Be careful, therefore, to understand where his major emphasis really is.

Third, the instructor bases his examination on subject matter drawn from all parts of the course. A professor of a comprehensive course on chamber music could scarcely ask only about Beethoven's last quartets. Be sure, therefore, that your review covers the whole course and that you do not merely concentrate on the parts of it you find interesting.

Finally, the kinds of questions which the instructor asks reflect his personal views on the examination procedure itself, as well as his competence in writing questions. Somebody once said that a teacher has only two choices: he can give essay questions and spend his life grading them, or he can give objective questions and spend his life constructing them. Try to find out which choice your own instructor has made. The art of writing examinations has progressed so far that objective questions (which used to be rather narrow and factual) can now be used to test for a wide range of goals. An essay examination has fewer questions, but they cover a broader range of material; also, the student must accept responsibility for the clear and coherent presentation of his ideas. In an objective examination, the student must ordinarily be sure to know about many more items, although the coverage of each may not be as deep as it is on an essay examination.

PREPARING FOR AN EXAMINATION

Certain childish habits are often associated with preparing for examinations. Among them are putting forth a great deal of frantic effort just before the examination, missing sleep, getting overstimulated by coffee or drugs, becoming too involved with other students in cram sessions, bragging about how hard you are working on your review, spending time talking about how tough the instructor is, worrying because other students seem to have a somewhat different approach, trying to outguess the instructor on which questions he will ask, and getting yourself into a generally worried and excitable frame of mind. Children do such things when they do not know how to study, and sometimes an adult will slip back into the bad ways of his youth. If you find yourself adopting this kind of behavior, take a good look at yourself and note ruefully that you are no longer a child and should not act like one.

Examinations are passed or failed long before you enter the examination room. Every student needs to study continually throughout a course. The best way to review is to go over what you have learned as soon as possible after you have studied it. Then periodically throughout the course you should refresh your memory on the successively larger bodies of knowledge which you have absorbed. No hasty, last-minute study can make up for the lack of earlier review. One experienced adult student put the matter in a highly expressive way: "Cramming for an exam is like trying to warm a cold room with a match."

A final review is essential. It enables you to develop a unity of viewpoint and to bring together in a meaningful whole everything you have learned. When you study a course, you begin by seeing its general shape, and you should never lose sight of it no matter how detailed your knowledge grows. When you come to the end, you should take time to look back again to fit all the knowledge together into a sufficient unity so that the essence of the course will remain in your mind forever. The final review and the examination are ways to help you do so.

The final review should be properly spaced. It should be completed at least a day in advance of the time you enter the examination room. The review itself can probably best occur in several sessions. If you do need to concentrate your review in a single session, be sure to allow yourself some rest periods during it. After the end of the final review, stop studying. You may need to check up on a few minor points, but be sure that they are few and that they are minor. Your mind will keep working on the course, either consciously or subconsciously, digesting, integrating, and synthesizing. This process will be aided rather than hampered if you put the examination out of your mind and go about your ordinary affairs. During this period, stay away from other students in the course. They will only confuse you. Keep to your normal and regular habits, getting as much food, sleep, and exercise as you usually do.

During the final review, be as active as possible in your approach to the material. You should first make a condensed summary or outline of the whole course so that once again you see its complete form. Here is how one student does this:

> Prior to the exam, I brief or outline all my classroom notes and reading notes. I then outline this outline and so on, thereby reducing the course to the basics. I find that in this manner I gain a good understanding of the course and can better reason out the problems presented in the exam.

After making this synthesis, look at the material of the course in as many different ways as you can.

1. Go back and do a straightforward review of all your notes, keeping in mind the basic outline which you have just made. At this point try to stay away from rereading the text or other material. You simply will not have time to do so. Instead, skim the textbook looking at the major headings and the central ideas which you have outlined.

2. Overlearn technical words, formulas, and principles so that they come automatically to you. You cannot comprehend the whole structure unless you know its basic terms and ideas. If on a final examination you must rethink a formula which you should have memorized, you will waste a great deal of time.

3. From your knowledge of the subject matter and your estimate of the parts of the course which your instructor believes to be most important, you should be able to guess what the major questions might be. Ask yourself these questions and think how you would answer them. Be careful not to restrict yourself only to them, however, for you cannot predict the full range of the questions which most instructors will ask. In any case, a study of only part of the material defeats your basic purpose which is to understand all of it.

4. Study as though you are going to be given an essay examination. G. Meyer [1] has reported an interesting experiment. A group of students were told they would have an objective test but were actually given an essay test. They did not do as well as students who had studied on the assumption that they would have an essay test. Then the situation was reversed. Students were told they would have an essay test but were actually given an objective test. They did just as well on it as the students who were told they would have an objective test. This result is not surprising. Essay questions make us call on all our resources of knowledge, and we are thereby helped to have a meaningful framework. Even though the objective questions may be highly specific, we can view them in context and therefore be helped to answer them.

5. Go back over your notes and concentrate particularly on any material which may be obscure to you or which you feel you have not mastered sufficiently.

6. If it is your ordinary practice to do so, study with other students or discuss the material with them. Even if you do not usually follow this practice, it might not

be a bad idea to schedule such a group session. Be careful, however, that it is really useful for you. Do not teach the material to somebody else, unless this practice gives you a fresh way of reviewing it. Be sure the discussion helps your thoughts to become clearer or more wide-ranging. If the group adopts any of the bad childhood patterns sometimes associated with studying for final examinations, withdraw from it. In any case, do not let the final part of your review for an examination be carried on with other people. Always reserve some time for independent study at the close of the review period.

7. At the very end, look back again at your master outline to get its fundamental structure in your mind. The last look at the cathedral or the course may be the most rewarding.

TAKING AN EXAMINATION

In any examination, two elements are always present: how much you know and how well you can present it in the limited time which you have available.

As you come to the examination, your mind should not be on yourself, your problems, and your worries but on the course and what you need to know. You should also try for the moment to hold your thoughts within the framework of the course itself. Adults know so many different things that they tend to see countless associations between what is taught in the course and the many aspects of life. While this practice is highly valuable in building learning associations, it may lead to an uncertain and too general approach to an examination. You will need to discipline your mind to deal only with the course itself and the particular approach of the instructor.

Before you go to an examination, be sure that you

have everything you will need in ample supply. For example, don't go with a ballpoint pen which has an almost empty cartridge or with an insufficient supply of paper. Be sure to take along a watch unless you know that you will have a clock immediately in view.

Go to the examination room in a leisurely fashion and get there ahead of time. The last minute rush and the frantic arrival will start you off in a poor frame of mind.

Do not do any last minute cramming outside the door of the examination room. It will only distort the pattern of your knowledge and tend to make you confused. If you talk with other students before the examination, try not to discuss either it or the content of the course.

In the examination room, choose the best possible seat—where you won't feel crowded, where there is ample space to work, and where you are least likely to be distracted. If you have had a regular seat during the course, use it also for the examination.

If at any time before or during the examination you find yourself getting a bit worried or panicky, consciously pause and concentrate on taking ten slow deep breaths. This process may or may not have any physiological effects, but it almost certainly has a sound psychological basis. Many students have found that the moment's preoccupation with deep breathing helps them greatly.

Plan your time during the examination. Divide the total amount available into three parts. You will need to allow a moment or so at the beginning to read the questions, the major part of the time to write your answers, and a little time at the end to review them. If it is a long examination, give yourself one or more brief rest periods in which you deliberately turn your mind away from what you are doing and concentrate on other matters.

Read all the questions on an examination before you tackle the early ones unless you are absolutely sure of your answers. The practice of reading all the questions gives you the total pattern of the examination and often provides practical help. You may find, for example, that the fifth question asks for material which otherwise you would put into the answer to the first question. A realization of this fact will save you from repeating yourself. Also, some of the later questions may give you ideas about how to answer the earlier ones.

Plan specifically the amount of time you will need in answering each question. If all the questions seem to have equal value, allot them equal time. If the instructor has indicated in any way that some questions are more important than others, divide up the time accordingly.

Be sure you really comprehend each question. Of all the rules for taking an examination, this one is the most important—and the most frequently violated. Instructors have usually tried very hard to help you by asking their questions in a way which they hope will lead or guide you to the correct answer. You may not realize this fact because no matter how calm you may think you are, you are bound to have a certain amount of tension. There is a tendency on the part of many students not to analyze the question which the instructor has painstakingly constructed but to leap ahead to give an answer which has little or no relevance to the question asked. Read every question at least twice before you answer, and note particularly any key words. For example, if the question asks you to "outline" something, use the outline form in your answer.

Be particularly careful not to put together the first few facts you hastily remember into a wrong synthesis. The student of English literature mentioned on page 72, for example, might misread the word "succeeds," identify Harry correctly as Henry V, remember the battle of Agincourt that he won, and therefore both misunderstand and misplace the quotation.

Answer the easy questions first. Doing so will give you confidence to tackle the harder questions.

If, after answering all the questions you know, you do get stuck on one, sit back and think of all the facts associated with it. Run over the basic outline of the course in your mind and try to see in what part of the outline the answer to that question seems to fall. If you think of any facts associated with this question or of any particular illustrations which the instructor has given, you may be helped to bring the answer back to your mind.

Finally, go over your paper at the end, reviewing and editing it. In this process look back at the questions once again to be sure that each answer is appropriate. There is no virtue in being the first person to leave the examination room and no stigma attached to being the last one there. Your second thoughts may greatly improve your performance, as second thoughts almost always do.

TAKING THE ESSAY EXAMINATION

In grading an essay examination, the examiner can look only at the words on the page. He cannot pay attention to your brilliant performance in class, to your outstanding earlier papers, or to your pleasing personality. He cannot read what was in your mind when you wrote your answer. All he can do is to look at what you have written and make a judgment about it.

One of the central purposes of an essay examination is to see how well the student can organize his thoughts and how effectively he can express them. The essay examination is just what its name implies. It is a series of brief essays on assigned subjects written under controlled conditions and with a limitation on time. In some sense, therefore, the instructor will apply precisely the same standards to the essay examination that he would to the essay which might be written as another requirement of the course.

Do not leap at once to answer an essay question. Instead, pause to organize your answer mentally, or on a piece of scratch paper, or, if it is not available, on the examination paper itself. Jot down very quickly the key ideas you plan to use in the order in which you are going to write them. Use key words and abbreviations so that you do not waste your time. Then write the answer to your question following the outline you have prepared as modified by any second thoughts you may have. If you have used the examination paper itself for the outline, be sure to cross it out before you turn in the paper.

In organizing your thoughts, it is often useful to put the central idea of your answer in the first paragraph or, if your essay is brief, in the first sentence. This fact will give the instructor confidence that you know what you are doing and a positive feeling about that particular answer. Also (it must be admitted), many instructors faced with large numbers of examination papers do not ponder every last word on each of them. An immediate and correct response in the first sentence or the first paragraph gives you a marked advantage.

State your answer as concretely as you can, using complete sentences. Do not merely sketch in a response, assuming that your instructor can fill in the blank places. Of course he can, but that is *your* job.

Do not pad your answer with all kinds of additional data or unnecessary facts. If you make a general point, it is good to give an illustration, thereby showing that you understand the practical applications of the subject. To give excessive illustrations, or to drag in other things you happen to know, however, is one of the most transparent efforts to try to fool an instructor—and he is seldom fooled.

Handwriting counts! The instructor usually tries to look only at the content of what you have written, but he cannot help being influenced by your presentation of your ideas. Illegible or childish penmanship, a disregard for even margins, and much rewriting and correcting always have a bad effect. Do your best during the examination, therefore, to express your ideas legibly and clearly so that your paper is as easy to read as possible.

Grammar counts, too! Write as carefully as you can to begin with and, in your editing, be sure to correct any mistakes you have made.

Leave enough room at the end of each answer so that you can go back later and add material to it. It often happens that while you are responding to another question, you will think of a useful point to add to an answer which you have already given. If you have not left space for such afterthoughts, you may have trouble squeezing them in. When you add extra bits at the end, your total answer will not be organized very logically and coherently, but your additional thoughts may prove to be important.

Answer every question. Even though you may not understand what the instructor is driving at, reflect about his question for a moment. Then write as clear and coherent an answer as you can manage. Sometimes your subconscious mind may help you to put down facts which have some relationship to what the instructor is asking you. In any case, there is nothing you can lose by answering. The least you can get on any question is a zero, and you will be sure to get it if the answer is blank.

This last rule does not apply, of course, if the instructor has told you not to answer questions unless you are sure of the answer or if the examination is intended to be so difficult that not even the ablest student can get all the answers. In either of these cases, you had better not answer unless you are sure you are right. A poor answer may be counted against you, or you may spread yourself so thin over many answers that you do not do well on any of them.

If you find that your mind is a complete blank on a question, do not simply sit and stare at it. On a sheet of scratch paper (or, if that is not available, on the examination paper itself), begin to jot down any ideas which occur to you. Even if the results are almost completely meaningless, you are *doing* something. The very process may calm you a bit. In many cases, however, it does much more than that. Because it starts a train of associations in your mind, the answer or some part of the answer may suddenly pop into your head. You can then sketch your outline and write your answer.

TAKING THE OBJECTIVE EXAMINATION

The most common kind of objective examination has multiple-choice items. Other basic forms of objective-type questions are those which call for matching various items with one another, for determining whether sentences are true or false, or for completing incomplete sentences. Other imaginative methods of objective-type examination have also been developed. One kind, for example, presents the student with a chart or graph and asks him a series of interrelated questions, or furnishes a paragraph of textual material and asks the student to apply his knowledge to the material it contains.

On these kinds of objective examinations, as well as on the more traditional ones, it is important to follow directions exactly. You must read and understand every word of the question. This point was made earlier, but it is particularly relevant to objective examinations.

If your instructions tell you not to guess on items, the instructor is probably indicating that wrong answers will be deducted from correct answers to get the total score. If you do guess incorrectly, therefore, your grade will be lower than it would be if you did not answer. If, on the other hand, you are not told you should not guess, it is usually wise to guess, since as was mentioned earlier, you will get a zero for an unanswered question anyway. If you guess, you may get the right answer, partly because you have a subconscious or partial memory which guides you correctly.

If you are instructed to study a paragraph or chart before answering certain questions, be sure to do so. Many students go at once to the questions and keep looking back and forth between them and the basic material, hoping to find the immediate responses to the specific questions asked. As a result, they reread the same material two or three times but never really absorb it. They are likely to answer incorrectly because they get the sense of only one sentence or one figure and not of the whole paragraph or chart.

When you have read the basic instructions, start through the examination paper, reading each question carefully and answering at once any item about which you are sure. When you have finished the paper, go through again and answer the other questions. As with any kind of examination, the later questions may throw light on the earlier ones. You may actually go over the paper several times before you get all the items answered.

Read closely all the words on the examination. There is a great deal of difference for example, between "usually" and "always"; "most" and "all"; "is" and "was"; and "many" and "few." Some students slur over important words and are therefore marked incorrect on an item when they actually know the correct answer.

It often happens that when a student edits his examination at the close of the hour, he feels uncertain about one of his original answers. Another now looks better to him. Should he change or should he not? F. K. Berrien [2], summarizing his research, says, "in harmony with the previous studies in this area, students in general are more likely to raise than lower their scores by changing answers on doubtful items." Berrien's suggestion is valid, however, only when the student is honestly torn by indecision about what is correct. If two answers seem plausible to him, he ought to choose the one which seems more correct, but if he has guessed the first time, there is no reason to believe that a second guess will be any better than the first.

AFTER THE EXAMINATION

If you are practicing with a rifle, you want to know whether you hit the target—and if not, why. In like fashion, you want to see your examination paper after it has been graded, and if you did not make the highest possible score, you want to know why. An instructor has an obligation to give you this information, though he may want to have you take the initiative in seeking it. In asking to see your paper or to discuss it with him, your attitude ought to be a positive one. You want to know how well you did and where you went off the track, so that you won't make the same mistake in the future. You are not challenging the instructor or doubting the adequacy of his grading.

On objective examinations, the instructor can ordinarily tell you fairly exactly where you made your mistakes. On essay examinations, he cannot do so with the same degree of accuracy. He has, perhaps, read thirty to fifty essays, all dealing with the same question, and has had to grade them in terms of his judgment of their relative quality. When your paper is presented separately, therefore, it may not be easy for him to tell you exactly what is wrong. If your score is only a few points below perfection, you should not expect that he will be able to provide this service for you. If your score falls very far below what you think it should be, however, there is clearly something wrong, and he should be able to tell you what it is.

An examination should be a learning experience from which you derive insight about the content of the course as well as about yourself. If you do not follow through after the examination, you will not get its full value.

CONCLUSION

At the end, as at the beginning, it should be stressed that the aim of this chapter has been only to give you help in getting your basic knowledge adequately appraised. You should not do yourself less than justice simply because you do not know how to take an examination. It is a great satisfaction to know. It is an even greater satisfaction to know that you know.

Chapter 10

A Lifetime
of Learning

In an African village at the edge of the Indian Ocean, there lives a chief with a great treasure. If you make your way to that remote spot, most of the villagers will crowd around you, eager to see a stranger, though a few of the women and children, equally curious but wary of danger, will take shelter and peer out at you from behind it. You will have difficulty in being heard among the confusion of voices. Presently, however, the chief will dart away into his hut and return bearing his treasure wrapped in oilcloth to keep away the damp and the insects.

When the folds of material have been carefully unwrapped, the treasure will be revealed. A book. A beginning reader, published long ago in England, with the faded cover torn away from the text and the pages blackened at the edges. As you turn it over and look at it, you will wonder what gives this ancient volume the value the chief so obviously believes it possesses? Does it have historical significance? Did it belong to Stanley or Livingstone?

The chief will take it from your hands. With a sharp command, he will silence the babble. Then, in the intent silence, he will open the book to the first page and begin to say the words aloud, pronouncing each one separately and so badly that you would not understand if you could not follow his finger. Presently, he will stop and hand the book back to you with a deep, beseeching gaze, pointing to the place where he stopped reading. Everything is suddenly clear. He wants you to teach him to say the next words. In this slow, painful way, with his ancient reader and the aid of an occasional wayfarer, he hopes to learn your language.

Into the mind of one visitor who had this experience, there flashed at that moment a piercing awareness both of the depth of man's longing for education and of the obstacles most men must overcome to satisfy that desire. That isolated chief is, in fact, more fortunate than most of the men and women now alive. He has one book. They have none.

Yet in some places in the world and particularly in the United States, so many opportunities to learn are so freely available that their variety is bewildering. Fifty years ago, the comedians Weber and Fields always got a laugh with their line, "You ought to be smart. You live next door to the school!" Today every American lives next door to so many schools that nobody has an excuse not to be smart.

Think of how many resources are now available to even the remotest farmer. The mail delivers all of the newspapers, magazines, government bulletins, and books he wishes to buy. He can usually borrow books free from his state library or university, or if he goes into the village, he can often get them from the traveling library or the book deposit station. His radio brings him an immediate involvement with the world's affairs. The extension service of his land-grant university helps him to organize programs for his further education. He can take correspondence courses from universities or private schools. He can borrow pictures and phonograph records from his state university, or he can build up a collection of his own. He and his neighbors can organize groups to buy shared books and records or to carry on a discussion program. In these and other ways is the answer given to the question asked long ago by the author of Ecclesiastes, "How can he get wisdom who holdeth the plow?"

And yet that farmer, all too often, will not use the resources available to him, and his brother who has gone to the city will not use the even richer opportunities which it offers. They have so many choices that finally they choose nothing. Meanwhile, both may go through life with a dull sense of dissatisfaction, feeling only partially awake and sensing that their mental and physical resources are being wasted. They do not realize what the African chief understands so well: the importance of education in building a better life. They need help, but they do not see that help lies close at hand.

WHERE TO TURN FOR INFORMATION AND ASSISTANCE

As you become aware of the basic idea of lifelong learning, you will be surprised to discover how many different opportunities are, in fact, available. National magazines, local newspapers, television, and radio carry advertisements for programs and describe successful efforts in various communities. The mail brings a steady stream of announcements of course offerings, educational events, magazine subscriptions, books, teaching machines, and other special materials. Churches, clubs, and other membership organizations sponsor activities for their members. Once you realize that these and many other endeavors are guided by the same purpose—to provide learning opportunities for adults—you become aware of the great possibilities for personal and social growth which modern society provides.

You must, of course, design your own pattern of activities, just as you decide other matters of personal concern, such as what clothes to wear, what food to eat, or where to go for a vacation. Your choice of educational activities is determined, in part at least, by where you live, because some communities have a much richer provision for learning opportunities than others. In many places, however, though not in all, there are institutions, programs, and services whose leaders are ready, and in most cases eager, to help any man or woman who seeks educational opportunities. It may be necessary to do a little exploring to find the right activity or the person who can help you most, but that exploration will be worthwhile. Here are some of the major local sources of assistance.

Check to see whether your community has an *adult education council*. This organization is usually made up of representatives of most of the major local programs. Often it has a fairly complete directory of educational opportunities or is prepared to advise and assist you to find them for yourself.

The *public library* is an excellent source of books and often of such other materials as phonograph records, films, pictures, and magazines. If it does not have what you want, its staff can ordinarily borrow books from other libraries. Also, many public libraries keep a special file of available educational opportunities. If you do not have a public library available, write to the state library to see whether it lends books directly or can tell you where to turn for help.

The *local school system* may offer evening courses or other kinds of learning opportunities. The program will usually have a director, and he is the person whom you should consult. If you cannot locate him, get directly in touch with the superintendent of schools, who can forward your inquiry so that it will receive prompt attention.

Most *colleges and universities* now offer at least modest programs for the people of their own communities and sometimes for a whole region or state. You might inquire of local institutions or of state or regional universities and colleges to see whether there is any extension, evening college, or continuing education division which can help you. If you fail to locate the proper source, get directly in touch with the president's office, which will be able to refer you to the proper authority.

All states have one or more land-grant universities which offer statewide educational services. If you would like to find out about them, inquire at your *county extension office.* In the past, the members of this staff have been chiefly concerned with agriculture and home economics for people in rural areas, but now the scope of service is being broadened to include many kinds of service for everyone.

Many communities have *museums,* and most of them have active educational programs. To find out about them, consult the educational director or the curator of the institution concerned.

Most cities have a variety of *community agencies,* such as YMCAs, YWCAs, community centers, and settlement houses, which provide general adult educational programs in classes, clubs, lectures, and other activities. Often, too, a church, a temple, or a synagogue will offer a forum or a group of classes for the general community.

City recreation departments or park authorities often have active educational programs. You can find out about them by writing or calling the proper authorities at the headquarters of such agencies.

Many businesses and industries have *directors of training* or *directors of personnel* who administer company educational activities and who also provide general counseling to employees on their educational programs.

Local unions may have educational programs sponsored by their *educational directors*.

Units of the armed services usually have *education officers* and *librarians,* both of whom are expected not only to operate their own basic services but also to guide servicemen and servicewomen toward other educational opportunities, including those provided by correspondence.

Television and radio stations often schedule courses or other special educational events. The stations may be willing to put you on a mailing list to receive regular announcements of broadcasts. In any case, make a practice of checking the schedules published daily in the newspapers so that you know about programs that would be profitable for you.

If you have access to a good *bookstore,* you will discover a great deal by browsing through its resources. You might find it useful, too, to come to know a particular salesclerk who can learn about your interests and help you get the books you want, even if they have to be especially ordered.

If you need more systematic and detailed guidance involving a number of interviews or a program of testing, you should seek a special *counseling center* which offers such services. Be sure that the center is operated on a professional basis by a qualified staff. Some centers are sponsored by universities, school systems, or other established community agencies. Some are operated privately; their fees are ordinarily higher than those of nonprofit institutions. Counseling centers are not widespread, and you may need to spend a period of time in a neighboring city if you wish to have this specialized kind of help.

Correspondence courses come from many different sources, but chiefly from universities, from private profit-making institutions, and from the armed services. The courses offered by universities are listed in a brochure called *Guide to Correspondence Study* available from the National University Extension Association, University of Minnesota. A list of the major private correspondence schools can be secured from the National Home Study Council, Washington. If you are in the armed services, consult your education officer concerning courses offered by the United States Armed Forces Institute as well as those sponsored by your particular branch of the service.

PRINCIPLES TO USE IN PLANNING YOUR STUDY

A lifetime of learning is now the privilege of everyone fortunate enough to live in a civilized society. The opportunities are rich enough so that each person can shape his program to suit his own desires and capacities. While no two people ever follow precisely the same pattern, experienced counselors at adult educational institutions suggest that there are some general principles which can be used by every man or woman to make or remake plans for study.

1. *Always have at least one "maintenance" activity.* Many adults realize that, while they once had sharp keen minds, they have not kept them active and alert. After years of inactivity, it is hard to start learning again. It takes a period of training to get back into condition, and many people do not feel that they can take the trouble to reestablish their skill.

The best solution for this problem is never to let the mind grow dull and limp. One young woman with seven children and no help in caring for them still finds time to carry out a resolution she made during her first pregnancy: to read thoroughly every week the Sunday edition of a great metropolitan newspaper. "Later on," she says, "I can get back to doing things more seriously and systematically. But when I do, I don't want to be twenty years behind the times and with a mind which has gone all soft and vague."

A maintenance activity requires continuing effort. One should do anything which seems best and most interesting. There are many possibilities. Read a serious magazine or book at least once a month. Complete one course in a class or by correspondence each year. Participate actively in the educational program of a club. Constantly be in the process of learning some new skill. Practice to extend the knowledge of a foreign language. Whatever activity is chosen, however, it should be continuously pursued.

When Charles Darwin [1] was a young man, he greatly enjoyed poetry, paintings, and music, but as he grew older, he turned his mind into what he called "a kind of machine for grinding general laws out of large collections of facts." As a result, he lost what he called "the higher tastes." "If I had to live my life again," he said late in life, "I would have made a rule to read some poetry and listen to some music at least once every week. . . ."

2. *If possible, carry on some group educational activity.* The value of shared learning has been fully explored in the preceding chapters of this book. Perhaps you cannot join a class or group every year, but try to do so as often as you can.

3. *Examine your personal problems to see how many of them can be met by education.* Not all of them can, to be sure. But one who sits back to take a long look at himself or discuss his situation with a friend or a professional counselor often concludes that he can make a better life for himself by learning more. "Do I want to get ahead on my job? If so, what do I need to learn in order to do so? Do I feel inadequate in social situations? If so, what groups can I join which will help me adjust to other people? Did I have an in-

adequate education in a subject I really need to understand? If so, how can I undergird my knowledge? Am I too narrow in my outlook? If so, what can I do to gain a broader view?" It is by asking and answering such questions that many adults start on their pathways to learning.

4. *Study enjoyable subjects in enjoyable ways.* Sometimes this principle goes counter to the one just mentioned, but if education can be a duty, it can also be a pleasure. When we are trying to solve a problem, the process is sometimes not a completely happy one, though, if possible, education should be thought of as a challenge and not as a chore. Often, however, one should begin to learn from a sense of interest and delight, broadening or deepening the knowledge of a favorite subject or taking part in a preferred activity. On the wall of the oracle of Delphi in ancient Greece were carved the words "Know thyself." In planning an educational program, it is wise to begin with oneself, and particularly with those things which are most satisfying and rewarding.

5. *Every now and then, try completely new subjects and new ways of learning.* The other inscription on the wall at Delphi was "Nothing too much." Why should anyone narrow his choice to only a few activities and spend all his time on them? There are ways to learn in many kinds of programs, and nobody can know which are best for him unless he tries a large number of them. One should never grow so old that he does not enjoy a new experience. If the Bible is right in allotting a lifetime span of three score years and ten, every adult has fifty years in which to keep on learning. It really isn't very long, but it does allow for a great deal of variety. One cannot do much to control the length of one's life, but one can do a great deal about its width and depth.

6. *Take full advantage of the flow of material which comes to you by the mass media.* Our own age is

characterized by an almost engulfing onrush of books, magazines, newspapers, films, phonograph records, plays, concerts, operas, radio and television programs, and other forms of communication aimed at large groups or even at the whole population of the country.

The book is the most flexibly useful of all instruments of mass learning. It can be a complete course of instruction in itself, or it can be combined with other books or materials into a larger sequence. It is inexpensive. It can be read at any time, either rapidly to get its gist or slowly to savor its richness. One can move back and forth through it as often as is desired, and it is easy to hold and to carry. It offers the opportunity to establish direct contact with the living and the dead. So many books are now in print that the range of choice is very great, far more than that available to any previous generation of mankind.

But each of the other mass media has its own distinctive values, and the discriminating learner keeps up with many of them. From the enormous variety available, he develops his own principles of choice to select only those instruments of learning or those experiences which will be most rewarding and most broadening for him.

7. *Take full advantage of the informal learning opportunities provided by your own community.* Many people establish surprisingly narrow patterns and pathways of life for themselves, moving back and forth in a restricted way between home, work, church, and recreation, scarcely being aware of what lies even a little way off their beaten path. One who deliberately sets forth to understand his city—its neighborhoods, its organizations, its differing patterns of value, its resources, and, most of all, the infinite variety of its people—will have a fascinating experience. One can travel widely in even a tiny village, as Henry David Thoreau [2] pointed out more than a hundred years ago.

One kind of local learning comes not from passive observation of a community but from active participation in its affairs. The conditions of life in our society are excellent for most people, but there are still many social frontiers to be crossed. It is both an exciting and a rewarding experience to work actively in organizations, to serve on boards, and to take part in community betterment programs. The insight which comes from such service is itself a highly satisfactory outcome— and it can be secured in no other way.

8. *Do not be restricted by the opportunities available in your own community.* Rewarding though community life may be, it is not sufficient to provide the broader horizon needed by most people today. Independent travel and organized study tours are growing in popularity. So is attendance at conferences, short courses, workshops, and summer camp meetings. Not only are such activities broadening and rewarding in themselves, but they also permit one to see himself and his community in a proper perspective.

These eight suggestions, and indeed this whole book, have been focused directly on the individual, suggesting some of the ways by which everyone can learn as well as some of the best methods for doing so. Every individual must answer for himself, in the light of his ability, his beliefs, and his way of life, the question: Why should I study at all? The answer, and the resulting pattern of learning, will change as he grows older. But every time a human being learns, he gains two values: first, the knowledge, the skill, the understanding, or the sensitivity itself, and second, the continuing reinforcement of his ability to learn as his mind and body are helped to stay strong and active.

The values of learning, while personally profitable, are not narrowly selfish. Both knowledge and the continuing growth of the mind are essential to society as well as to the individual. Kingdoms and kingly eras were judged by the ability and the wisdom of the king. In a democracy, the people themselves rule—and therefore democracies and democratic eras must be judged by the ability and the wisdom of the people.

REFERENCES

Chapter 1

1. Rene Descartes, *Les Principes De La Philosophie,* Publiées Par Victor Cousin, Chez F. G. Levrault, Paris, 1824, vol. 3, pp. 21–22. The complete text reads as follows:

   ... je voudrois qu'on le parcourût d'abord tout entier ainsi qu'un roman, sans forcer beaucoup son attention ni s'arrêter aux difficultés qu'on y peut rencontrer, afin seulement de savoir en gros quelles sont les matières dont j'ai traité; et qu'après cela, si on trouve qu'elles méritent d'être examinées et qu'on ait la curiosité d'en connoître les causes, on le peut lire une seconde fois pour remarquer la suite de mes raisons; mais qu'il ne se faut pas derechef rebuter si on ne la peut assez connoître partout, on qu'on ne les entende pas toutes; il faut seulement marquer d'un trait de plume les lieux où l'on trouvera de la difficulté et continuer de lire sans interruption jusqu'à la fin; puis, si on reprend le livre pour la troisième fois, j'ose croire qu'on y trouvera la solution de la plupart des difficultés qu'on aura marquées auparavant, et que, s'il en reste encore quelques unes, on en trouvera enfin la solution en relisant.

2. Howard Yale McClusky, "An Experiment on the Influence of Preliminary Skimming on Reading," *The Journal of Educational Psychology,* vol. 25, pp. 521–529, 1935.

3. Walt Whitman, "Democratic Vistas," *Complete Prose Works,* David McKay Publisher, Philadelphia, 1892, p. 257.

Chapter 2

1. Sherman B. Sheffield, "The Orientations of Adult Continuing Learners," unpublished doctoral dissertation, Department of Education, The University of Chicago, Chicago, 1962.
2. Virginia Voeks, *On Becoming an Educated Person*, 2d ed., W. B. Saunders Company, Philadelphia, 1964.
3. Benjamin P. Thomas, *Abraham Lincoln*, Alfred A. Knopf, Inc., New York, 1960, p. 500. Permission to use this quotation granted by Alfred A. Knopf, Inc.
4. Oscar Wilde, quoted by Hesketh Pearson, *Oscar Wilde, His Life and Wit*, Harper & Row, Publishers, Incorporated, New York, 1946, p. 325.
5. *Selection from the Correspondence of the Late Mac-Vey Napier, Esq.*, The Macmillan Company, New York, 1879, pp. 98–99.
6. Sydney Smith, quoted by Peter Quennell, *The New Statesman and Nation*, vol. 8, new series, no. 183, p. 241, Aug. 25, 1934.
7. Seneca, *Ad Lucilium Epistulae Morales*, Epistle LXXVI, Harvard University Press, Cambridge, Mass., 1917, vol. 2, p. 150.
8. Luella Cole Pressey, "The Permanent Effects of Training in Methods of Study on College Success," *School and Society*, vol. 28, pp. 403–404, 1928.
9. As Mr. Kettering himself observed, he told this story often and in different forms. One version appears in the book of his speeches entitled *Prophet of Progress*, E. P. Dutton & Co., Inc., New York, 1961, p. 18. The version used here, provided long ago by a friend, seems more immediately relevant than the others found in Mr. Kettering's writings.

Chapter 3

1. Irma T. Halfter, "Aging and Learning: An Achievement Study," *The School Review*, vol. 70, pp. 287–302, 1962.

2. Jerome S. Bruner and Cecile C. Goodman, "Value and Need as Organizing Factors in Perception," *The Journal of Abnormal and Social Psychology*, vol. 42, pp. 33–44, 1947.

3. John Stuart Mill, *The Subjection of Women*, Henry Holt and Company, New York, 1898, p. 313.

4. Henry Van Dyke, quoted by Willis H. Reals, *Better Teaching, Better Learning*, Washington University Press, St. Louis, 1961.

Chapter 4

1. E. G. Williamson, "The Relationship of Number of Hours of Study to Scholarship," *The Journal of Educational Psychology*, vol. 26, p. 687, 1935. Permission to use this quotation granted by Abrahams Magazine Service, Inc.

2. H. A. Peterson, Mary Ellis, Norine Toohill, and Pearl Kloess, "Some Measurements of the Effects of Reviews," *The Journal of Educational Psychology*, vol. 26, pp. 65–72, 1935.

3. F. C. Rose and S. M. Rostas, "The Effect of Illumination on Reading Rate and Comprehension of College Students," *The Journal of Educational Psychology*, vol. 37, p. 290, 1946. Permission to use this quotation granted by Abrahams Magazine Service, Inc.

4. Mack T. Henderson, Anne Crews, and Joan Barlow, "A Study of the Effect of Music Distraction on Reading Efficiency," *The Journal of Applied Psychology*, vol. 29, pp. 313–317, 1945.

Chapter 5

1. Francis P. Robinson, *Effective Study*, rev. ed., Harper & Row, Publishers, Incorporated, New York, 1961.

2. W. A. Barton, "Outlining as a Study Procedure," *Teachers College Contributions to Education*, no. 411, 1930.

3. William James, *The Principles of Psychology,* Henry Holt and Company, New York, 1890, vol. 1, p. 662.
4. William Frederick Book, "The Psychology of Skill with Special Reference to Its Acquisition in Typewriting," *University of Montana Publications in Psychology,* vol. 1, bulletin no. 53, pp. 90–100, 1908.
5. F. W. Bourdillon, "The Night Has a Thousand Eyes," *A Victorian Anthology,* edited by Edmund Clarence Stedman, Houghton Mifflin and Company, New York, 1895, p. 533.

Chapter 6
1. John W. Gardner, "National Goals in Education," *Goals for Americans,* Prentice Hall Inc., Englewood Cliffs, N.J., 1960, p. 86.
2. Francis Bacon, "Of Studies," *The Works of Francis Bacon,* collected and edited by James Spedding, Robert Leslie Ellis, and Douglas Denon Heath, Longman & Company, London, 1858, vol. 6, p. 498.
3. Patrick Meredith, *Learning, Remembering, and Knowing,* Association Press, New York, 1961, p. 118. Permission to use this quotation granted by Association Press.
4. Gerard Manley Hopkins, "Pied Beauty," *Poems of Gerard Manley Hopkins Now First Published,* edited with notes by Robert Bridges, Oxford University Press, London, 1918, p. 30. Permission to reprint this poem granted by Oxford University Press.
5. Edith Hamilton, *The Greek Way,* W. W. Norton & Company, Inc., New York, 1942, pp. 15–16. Permission to use this quotation granted by W. W. Norton & Company, Inc.
6. Winston S. Churchill, *My Early Life, A Roving Commission,* Thornton Butterworth Limited, London, 1930, p. 31.
7. Paul D. Leedy, *Reading Improvement for Adults,* McGraw-Hill Book Company, Inc., New York, 1956,

p. 432. Permission to use this quotation granted by McGraw-Hill Book Company, Inc.

8. Paul Witty, "The Improvement of Reading Abilities," *Adult Reading*, Fifty-fifth Yearbook of the National Society for the Study of Education, 1956, part 2, p. 251. Permission to use this quotation granted by NSSE.

9. William S. Gray and Bernice Rogers, *Maturity in Reading*, The University of Chicago Press, Chicago, 1956.

Chapter 7

1. Epictetus, *The Discourses as Reported by Arrian, The Manual, and Fragments*, G. P. Putnam's Sons, New York, 1926, vol. 1, "Discourses, Book II," p. 348.

2. Porter G. Perrin, *Writer's Guide and Index to English*, 3d ed., Scott, Foresman and Company, Chicago, 1959.

3. Rudolph Flesch, *The Art of Readable Writing*, Harper & Row, Publishers, Incorporated, New York, 1959.

4. Arthur Thomas Quiller-Couch, *On the Art of Writing*, G. P. Putnam's Sons, New York, 1961.

5. Benjamin Franklin, *Autobiography*, R. R. Donnelley and Sons Company, Chicago, 1903, pp. 19–20.

6. Alexander Pope, *An Essay on Criticism*, 7th ed., printed for Bernard Lintot, London, 1728, p. 20.

Chapter 8

1. Ben Jonson, *Discoveries*, E. P. Dutton & Co., Inc., New York, 1923, p. 5.

2. Lester A. Kirkendall, "Factors Inhibiting Pupil Questioning in Class," *Educational Method*, vol. 16, pp. 359–362, 1937.

3. Francis P. Robinson, *Effective Study*, rev. ed., Harper & Row, Publishers, Incorporated, New York, 1961.

4. Benjamin Franklin, *Autobiography*, R. R. Donnelley and Sons Company, Chicago, 1903, pp. 22–23.

Chapter 9

1. George Meyer, "An Experimental Study of the Old and New Types of Examination," *The Journal of Educational Psychology*, vol. 25, pp. 641–661, 1934; vol. 26, pp. 30–40, 1935.
2. F. K. Berrien, "Are Scores Increased on Objective Tests by Changing the Initial Decision?" *The Journal of Educational Psychology*, vol. 31, p. 67, 1940. Permission to use this quotation granted by Abrahams Magazine Service, Inc.

Chapter 10

1. Charles Darwin, *The Autobiography of Charles Darwin*, Nora Barlow, editor, Collins Clear-Type Press, London, 1958, p. 139.
2. Henry David Thoreau, *Walden, or, Life in the Woods*, Houghton Mifflin Company, New York, 1893.

INDEX